WIVES, SLAVES,
AND
SERVANT GIRLS

WIVES, SLAVES, AND SERVANT GIRLS

ADVERTISEMENTS for *FEMALE RUNAWAYS* in AMERICAN NEWSPAPERS, 1770-1783

DON N. HAGIST

Illustrations by Eric H. Schnitzer

WESTHOLME
Yardley

Westholme Publishing, LLC

904 Edgewood Road

Yardley, Pennsylvania 19067

Visit our Web site at www.westholmepublishing.com

First Printing April 2016

10 9 8 7 6 5 4 3 2 1

ISBN: 978-1-59416-252-7

Also available as an eBook.

Printed in the United States of America

For the countless thousands of wives, slaves, and servant girls who never ran away, who were never advertised, and who are not remembered by history.

CONTENTS

INTRODUCTION

L OST AND FOUND. RAN AWAY AND TAKEN UP. In an era when
people could be considered property, either in terms of con-
tractual obligation or explicit ownership, it was natural for their
loss to be advertised and for owners to be sought when fugitives
were found. Notice could be circulated by word of mouth or hand-
bills, but the vast majority of advertisements that survive were
posted in newspapers. Almost every issue of every newspaper in
eighteenth-century America included at least one advertisement
for a runaway, mixed in with ads for lost horses, livestock, and
goods, and interspersed with commercial and legal notices. Slaves,
servants, deserters, absconded spouses, and thieves were sought by
owners, masters, officers, and other claimants hoping to recover
the individual or the property they had taken. These advertisements offer a remarkable look at a segment of society that is rarely
examined in detail, and yet which composed a substantial portion
of the population.

The ads are compelling in that, to be effective, they attempt to
distinguish a single person from the general population without
the aid of photographs or images. They list common attributes
like height and hair color, and distinctive characteristics such as
scars, birthmarks, deformities, speech patterns, and habits. These
verbal renderings reveal a range of individuals employed in the
myriad menial roles that made up the working and lower classes —
those who lived in anonymity unless they were bold enough to flee

their situation. Often the fugitive's clothing is described, and the details about fabrics, colors, patterns, and condition provide valuable information about regional clothing styles and material culture. The phrase "had on and took with" appears frequently, making it uncertain what was the runaway's personal property but indicating how much a person was liable to carry on a journey. It gives us a sense of what garments and goods were considered either valuable or important to possess, and illustrates the variety of garments in use during the era. Each description of personal attributes, clothing, possessions, and circumstances reveals an individual about whom, in most cases, we know nothing except what survives in the advertisement. Their peers who dutifully remained at their stations, on the other hand, are for the most part completely unknown to us.

Other volumes have been published containing collections of advertisements for runaway slaves, and for military deserters. This volume is focused on females, containing 400 advertisements for women and girls who were reported as runaways during the era of the Revolutionary War. The ads are an excellent primary source for descriptions of clothing, accessories, and other aspects of material culture. Throughout the eighteenth century, advertisements for men outnumber those for women by about ten to one. During the Revolutionary War years, (1775–1783), there are significantly fewer ads for runaways in general and female runaways in particular when compared to the previous five years. This may be because of the ineffectiveness of such ads during wartime rather than an actual change in the numbers of runaways. The chaos of war presented an opportunity for people to run away, and drastically diminished the chances of them being caught, so the idea of spending money on an advertisement for a runaway's capture may have been less appealing. While ads for runaways in general declined, ads for army deserters became common during the war.

An attempt was made to present a regionally balanced sample, but the primary source information is not distributed evenly among the American colonies. Some colonies had several newspapers in print regularly, while others had no newspapers, or very irregular production. Complete runs of some newspapers are not available. Some newspapers carried more ads for runaways than others: newspapers in Pennsylvania routinely included far more runaway ads than newspapers from other colonies. An issue of the *Pennsylvania Gazette* might contain ten or twelve such advertisements, while papers from Massachusetts, Rhode Island, and Virginia published the same week might contain only one. There are several possible reasons for this uneven distribution of runaway ads, but the result is that we have many more descriptions of women who ran away from the mid-Atlantic colonies than from those in the north or south.

There is no way to determine how effective these advertisements were, but throughout the eighteenth century and well into the nineteenth, runaway ads appeared in nearly every newspaper, so their expense must have been justified by an expectation of results. They offered rewards for the return of the runaway and stolen goods; reimbursement of expenses incurred by the captor were often offered as well. The prevalence of these advertisements is a testimony to the value of their subjects and indicates that it was cheaper to recover someone than to replace them.

The wording of each ad presented here is copied verbatim from the original. The text has been formatted for a book rather than for newspaper columns, and font and capitalization have been standardized rather than mimicking the original ad layout. Original spellings have been retained. Some original ads had blank spaces, probably due to mistakes in typesetting or inking; in these cases, the spelling or punctuation has been corrected. When the place of publication is not obvious from the newspaper's title, it is given in parentheses after the title. A Virginia statute required that all newspapers published in that colony be named *The Virginia Gazette*; to distinguish the different versions, the publisher's name is given before the title.

The terminology used to describe clothing in these ads was extensive and varied. A glossary appears at the end of this volume, in which most of the terms are defined. The definitions presented here are brief and are intended only for general guidance; many of the terms used for fabrics in the eighteenth century were imprecise, and some usages varied from region to region. We also assume that the advertisers knew the proper terminology for the garments and fabrics they described, which may not be the case. The wide range of terms used shows us not only the great variety of fabrics and styles available in the colonies, but also their importance as a descriptive feature. It is remarkable that the advertisers could remember so many details, and that readers could be expected to recognize these details in people that they encountered.

The descriptive nature of runaway ads makes them a treasure trove for those seeking to learn more about working and lower class women during the Revolutionary War era. Poor women didn't sit for portraits, and their lives were not chronicled in diaries and letters. These ads give us something of a portrait of them, and while they were placed to recover those women who were bold enough, incorrigible enough, or brave enough to run away, they can still provide insights into the character and circumstances of all lower class women at the time: not just those who ran, but also those who stayed behind, and labored in anonymity to help build a fledgling nation.

This book was originally published in 2007 by Ballindalloch Press as *Wenches, Wives and Servant Girls*. This new edition includes a new introduction, further reading, and corrections to errors. The advertisements in this volume are the same as in the previous edition, except for the replacement of five that were accidentally duplicated in the earlier edition.

The original edition was made possible by the support of Paul Dickfoss, Eric Schnitzer and Mark Tully. Special thanks to Jennifer Klein for encouragement and support throughout the development of this edition.

FURTHER READING

Blacks Who Stole Themselves: Advertisements for Runaways in the Pennsylvania Gazette, 1728-1790. Billy G. Smith and Richard Wojtoowicz. Philadelphia: University of Pennsylvania Press, 1989.

"Drinks hard, and swears much" White Maryland Runaways, 1770-1774. Joseph Lee Boyle. Baltimore, MD: Clearfield Publishing, 2010.

Had On and Took With Her: Clothing in Female Runaway Servant Advertisements from the Pennsylvania Evening Post, 1774-1784. Sue Huesken and Karen Mullian. Palmyra, NJ: SK Shortgown Research, 1995.

"He loves a good deal of rum…" Military Desertions during the American Revolution, 1775-1783. Joseph Lee Boyle. 2 Volumes. Baltimore, MD: Clearfield Publishing, 2009.

"Pretends To Be Free": Runaway Slave Advertisements from Colonial and Revolutionary New York and New Jersey. Graham Russell Hodges and Alan Edward Brown, eds. New York: Garland Publishing, 1994.

Runaway Slave Advertisements: A Documentary History from the 1730s to 1790. 4 Volumes. Lathan A. Windley. Westport, CT: Greenwood Press, 1983.

Runaways, Deserters, and Notorious Villains From Rhode Island Newspapers. 2 Volumes. Maureen Alice Taylor and John Wood Sweet, eds. Camden, ME: Picton Press, 1995 and 2001.

1770

[1] Run away from the Subscriber, living at the White plains, in the Manor of Cortlandt, the twenty-fourth of November last, a Mustee Wench, Servant to John Underhill, named Lucey; she is very well set and pretty fat: Had on when she went away, a long Gown with ruffled Cuffs, and several striped Pettycoats, and a black Hat. Whoever takes up the said Wench, and brings her to the Subscriber, shall receive Forty Shillings Reward, and all reasonable Charges, paid by John Underhill. [*New York Gazette*, January 1, 1770]

[2] New Castle county, December 28, 1769. Now in the goal of said county, a certain Elizabeth Berry, about 20 years of age, born in Ireland, a low thick set woman, fair complexion, brown hair, and speaks much like an English woman; she says she served her time with Jacob Philimon, in Frederick county, Maryland; had on, when committed, a linsey coat, and coarse homespun shift, without shoes or stockings. Also Thomas Bolton, born in England, about 30 years of age, 5 feet 2 or 3 inches high, brown hair, and red beard, by trade a taylor; had on, and with him, when committed, two suits of cloaths, one of a light cloth colour, and one blue, the waistcoat of the latter, full trimmed, with yellow gilt buttons. Likewise Mary Watson, born in Ireland, 25 years of age, fair complexion, sandy hair, and a little pock marked; had on, when committed, a striped stuff gown, a purple calicoe ditto, high heeled leather shoes, white metal buckles, and worsted stockings; says she

came into this country with Captain Burn, about two years ago, and belongs to John Doyle, of the city of Philadelphia. Likewise a Negroe man, named Cuff, about 25 years of age; he says he was born in Barbados, and lived with Jonathan Smith, of Philadelphia; had on, when committed, a blue waistcoat, with a short swanskin ditto, long trowsers, and brown great coat; his cloathes much worn. Since his confinement, says he belongs to Thomas Saven, in Maryland. Their masters, if any they have, are desired to come and pay their charges, in six weeks from the date, and take them away, or they will be sold for the same, by Thomas Pusey, Goaler. [*Pennsylvania Gazette*, January 11, 1770]

[3] Run away from the subscriber, on or about the 6th of December last, an indented servant man named James Russell, about 5 feet 7 or 8 inches high, had on when he went away a blue cloth coat lapelled, a light coloured frize jacket which he puts on by turns, striped ticken breeches, and might have had others, worsted stockings, and part worn shoes; he has a remarkable scar on the left side of his chin, has lost one or two of his fore teeth, which causes him to lisp, or rather to have a stoppage in his speech. He left me in Currituck county, North Carolina, and suppose that he is now lurking about or at Princess Anne. Also a servant woman named Anne Thompson, of a middle size, tolerably lusty, and black hair; she had on an old check bedgown, linsey woolsey petticoat and old shoes. Whoever brings either of said servants unto Mr. Joseph Calvert, Mrs. Pullett, or Mr. Shoemaker, at Mr. Walke's, shall receive for the man Four Dollars, and for the woman Two Dollars, and all reasonable charges paid, by me George Woolsey. [Rind's *Virginia Gazette*, February 8, 1770]

[4] November 25, 1768. Run away from the subscriber, living in Bedminster township, Bucks county and Province of Pennsylvania, a Dutch servant man, named Adam Myer, about 25 years of age, well set, is much seamed and disfigured with the small-pox: Had on when he went away a blue Dutch made coat and jacket, with a great quantity of buttons on both: He left me in six weeks after he landed, and it is supposed, is gone towards New-York. Also, October 24, 1769. Run away from the sub-

scriber, a Negro woman named Sarah, about 40 years of age, somewhat marked with the small pox, has two teeth remarkably broad; speaks good Low Dutch and English, took some clothes with her, and had on good shoes tied with strings, and it is thought is gone towards N. York: Whosoever will secure the above described servant man in any gaol so as his master shall have speedy notice, shall have a reward of six pounds; if taken out of the province and brought home, eight pounds Pennsylvania currency; and for the Negro woman if she is secured in any of his Majesty's gaols so as I shall have her again, shall have a reward of one pound ten shillings Pennsylvania currency, by me John Bos. [*New York Journal*, February 15, 1770]

[5] Run away from the subscriber, in Charles City county, the 22d of December last, a Virginia born Negro woman named Edith, about 40 years of age, 5 feet 9 or 10 inches high, of a yellowish complexion, and two of her toes grow together, but on which foot I don't remember. She had on when she went away a striped Virginia cloth petticoat and waistcoat, and can read pretty well. It is likely she has changed her dress, as she carried sundry other cloaths with her, and a new Dutch blanket. Whoever takes up the said runaway, and conveys her to me, shall have Twenty Shillings reward, if taken in this county, and Thirty Shillings if taken out of it. Nicholas Holt. [Rind's *Virginia Gazette*, March 22, 1770]

[6] Thirteen Pounds Reward. Run away, on Saturday the 10th instant, from the subscribers, living in Baltimore town, Maryland, the following servants, viz. John Chambers, an English convict servant man, about 21 years of age, 5 feet 7 or 8 inches high, of a pale complexion, gray eyes, and bandy legs; had on and took with him sundry suits of clothes, nine ruffled shirts, a brown bush wig, a pair of single channel boots, a blue cloth great coat, and 150 l. cash, which he robbed his masters house of on the night of his elopement. Margaret Grant, a mulatto, about 20 years of age, 5 feet 1 or 2 inches high; had on and took with her sundry womens apparel, but has since disguised herself in a suit of mens blue cloth clothes, attending as waiting boy on the above John Chambers. She is an artful hussy, can read and write, has been in Barbados,

Antigua, the Grenades, Philadelphia, and says she was born in Carolina. Whoever apprehends the said servants, and secures them and the money, so that their masters may have them again, shall have the above reward, and reasonable charges, if brought home, paid by Henry James. Mordecai Gist. [Purdie & Dixon's *Virginia Gazette,* April 5, 1770]

[7] Run away, on the 27th of March, from the subscriber, living in Charlestown township, Chester county, in Pennsylvania, a servant girl, named Rebecca Cawood, about 14 years of age, well grown, swarthy complexion, light brown hair, down look, walks clumsey; had on, and took with her, a linsey jacket, patched under the arms, with patches of a different colour, and two short loose gowns, the one striped linsey, the other striped linen, three linsey petticoats, one of them new, black yarn stockings, good shoes, with leather heels, and tied with strings, a new black whalebone bonnet, and an old brown short cloak. Whoever takes up and secures said servant, so that her master may have her again, shall have Four Dollars reward, and if brought home reasonable charges, paid by me Jonathan Wells. [*Pennsylvania Gazette*, April 12, 1770]

[8] Run away from the Subscriber, living in Salisbury Township, Lancaster County, in the Night of 10th inst. April, a native Irish Servant Woman, named Margaret Welsh, about 22 Years of Age, about 5 Feet two Inches high, fresh Complexion, and brown Hair; had on, and took with her, one Calicoe Gown, double purple, about half worn; on the right Skirt two small pieces set in; two short Gowns, one Calicoe, pieced before with a Piece not the same with the Gown; one striped Linen, blue and white, two Linsey Petticoats, the one striped, the other brown, one fine Lawn Apron, one old Check ditto, one large Kenting Handkerchief, with a flowered Border, one Thread flowered Gause Ditto, two Pair of Stockings, the one Thread, the other Worsted, two Pair old Shoes, the one Leather, the other Cloth, with Brass Buckles; a Leghorn Hat, and sundry Things unknown. Whoever takes up said Servant, and secures her in any Goal, so as she may be had again, shall have Thirty Shillings Reward, and reasonable Charges, paid by Sarah Hopkins. [*Pennsylvania Gazette*, April 19, 1770]

Rebecca Cawood, fourteen-year-old servant, wears "a linsey jacket, patched under the arms," a linsey petticoat, "a new black whalebone bonnet," and "good shoes . . . tied with strings;" she carries "an old brown short cloak." See advertisement 7 from the *Pennsylvania Gazette*, April 12, 1770. Illustration by Eric H. Schnitzer.

[9] Four Dollars Reward. Run away, the 24th of April last, from the subscriber, living in Salisbury township, Lancaster county, a servant girl, named Anne Mackey, about 18 or 19 years of age, born in Ireland, speaks much on that country dialect, a stout chunky girl, dark brown hair, a coarse homespun shift, an old black and white striped linsey short gown, two linsey petticoats, one striped, the other a walnut colour, old leather heeled shoes. Whoever secures said servant, so as her master may have her again, shall have the above reward of Four Dollars, and reasonable charges, paid by Jarred Graham. [*Pennsylvania Gazette*, May 3, 1770]

[10] Run away from the Subscriber, living in Broad-Street, on Saturday the 28th of April last, a yellow Skin Negro Wench, named Bellow, born in Barbados, about 23 Years of Age, of a middle Stature: Had on when she went away, a blue striped Homespun Petticoat, a blue Coating Waistcoat, lined with Oznabrugs, a blue Cotton Romall Handkerchief tied about her Head, and a red and white cross bar'd Handkerchief round her Neck, without Shoes or Stockings. Whoever will apprehend and bring the said Negro Wench to her Master, shall have Five Dollars Reward; and whoever harbours or conceals her, may rest fully assured of having the Severity of the Law put in force against them. Richard Harris. [*New York Gazette*, May 7, 1770]

[11] Ran away from the Subscriber, living in Port-Tobacco, the 8th Day of May last, a likely Negro Wench, named Nann, about Five Feet high, very spare: Had on, when she went away, a stampt Cotton Gown, a ditto Petticoat Cross-barr'd and an old blue Camlet Mantle lined with stampt Cotton: is much pitted with the Small-Pox. Has a very brazen Look, and remarkable thick Lips; she has a red Spot on one of her Eyes, and a very fine Set of Teeth, and talks broad. She formerly belonged to Mr. Edward Smoot. Whoever takes up the said Negro Woman, and brings her to the Subscriber, shall receive Twenty Shillings Reward, besides what the Law allows. Joseph Sims, Son of Francis. [*Maryland Gazette*, June 21, 1770]

[12] Run away from the subscriber some time in November last, a Mulatto woman of a middle size, though slim; she has the appearance of moth upon her cheeks, her hands very remarkable, as she cannot straiten her fingers. Her dress, when she went away, was a Negro cotton petticoat and jacket, oznabrig shift, and a pair of old shoes, but I imagine she has altered her dress. She was seen about Christmas at the upper end of this county, and went by the name of Free Fanny; since this I have never heard of her, therefore suppose she passes for a free woman. Whoever apprehends the said woman, and brings her home, shall have a reward of Thirty Shillings, if taken up in Essex, and if in another county Fifty Shillings, and if in another government Five Pounds, paid by Henry Purkins. [Rind's *Virginia Gazette*, July 12, 1770]

[13] Run Away this morning, being a second time, from Thomas Younghusband, a Negro wench named Lydia (the property of Isaac and Israel Younghusband) about 18 years of age, 5 feet 4 or 5 inches high, stockey and well made, and has a likely face; had on when she went away a white osnabrug jacket and petticoat. I am pretty sure she is gone to Williamsburg, as she was before taken up on that road. Whoever apprehends the said Negro, and brings her to me, or secures her in any of his Majesty's jails, so that I get her again, shall have 3 l. Reward. Thomas Younghusband. [Purdie & Dixon's *Virginia Gazette*, July 19, 1770]

[14] Run away from the subscriber, in the night of the 26th instant, two Irish servants, Terrance Gaffney and Jane his wife, aged about 30 years each. I bought them last July, of Mr. James Porter in Maryland. The man has a white twilled suit of clothes, made this summer, two old cloth coats, two new white sheeting shirts, and some old ones. He stole a pair of new shoes, made in the best manner, also a pair of Virginia thread stockings, with part of their feet of cotton, and an old fine hat lined with brown holland. He is of a middle size, and wears dark short hair, that curls around, and he speaks remarkably hoarse. He understands waiting in a house and dressing hair. Jane has a thin visage, and wears gold bobs with stones in them, and black calimanco shoes, with plated buckles, white cotton stockings, an old calico gown, and a very

large scarlet cloak. Whoever secures the said servants, so that I get them, shall have 40s. reward, besides what the law allows. James Edmondson. [Purdie & Dixon's *Virginia Gazette,* August 16, 1770]

[15] Four Dollars Reward. Run away, on the 17th of August, 1770, from the subscriber, living in Queen Anne's county, near Queen's Town, Maryland, an English servant woman, named Catherine Marsh, of a middle size, much pock marked, has yellowish hair, aged about 22 years, or thereabouts; had on, when she went away, a striped linsey quilted petticoat, a home made linen short gown, with pale stripes, a home made linen shift, and a small black silk hat, much wore. The above servant arrived in Philadelphia on Friday, the 24th of August, late in the evening and was taken up on the 28th in the morning, but was rescued on Market street wharff, by some fellows unknown, and is supposed to be about that city or suburbs yet. Whoever takes up said servant, and brings her to me, or secures her, shall have the above reward, and reasonable charges, paid by me Peter Denny. [*Pennsylvania Gazette*, September 6, 1770]

[16] Chester, September 5, 1770. This day was committed to my custody as a runaway, a Negroe man, named Abel, who says he is a slave to Thomas Butler, in Cumberland county, who lives within about 10 miles of Carlisle; his master is desired to come and pay charges, and take him away, by Joseph Thomas, Goaler. Also was committed to my custody, on the 22d day of August last, a Woman, who calls herself Mary Sanderson, alias Heyney, for stealing clothes from sundry persons, which have been owned; and as there are many clothes still in my custody, supposed to be stolen, viz. 3 good shifts, of about a 900 linen, 2 linen handkerchiefs, one lawn, 2 muslin and 1 cambrick ditto, 2 holland aprons, 1 long lawn, 2 home made linen ditto and 1 linen petticoat, 2 pair of India calicoe pockets, 2 white linen short gowns, a pink coloured calimancoe quilt, a lincey jacket and petticoat, with two sorts of stripes in the petticoat, and several plaid or linen and yarn stockings; whoever has lost the said clothes, proving their property, may have them again, by applying in six weeks from the date hereof, or they will be disposed of according to law, by Joseph Thomas, Goaler. [*Pennsylvania Gazette,* September 13, 1770]

[17] Absconded from her master's service, on Sunday the 15th of July last, an English servant girl, named Patty, or Martha Jones; she is a thin small girl, supposed to be about 20 years of age; her eyes are so remarkably small and the eye-lids so much contracted, that to a stranger she will appear as almost blind. Had on and took away with her, a dark cotton gown, two striped linsey petticoats, two white aprons, one white striped kenting handkerchief, one new bandano ditto, a black sattin bonnet lined with blue persian, one pair of white stockings, and a pair of old black worsted shoes. She came from Bristol about a year since, in the Hercules, Capt. Scott, was seen at Kensington where the vessel lay the next day after, and at Spring Garden the day after that, the next day was at the Nag's-Head Tavern on the Reading road, and tarried there all night, saying she had leave from her mistress to look for another master. I have reason to believe she is somewhere on the road between Schuykill, and the Nag's Head, or perhaps has gone up the Reading road. Whoever will send or bring said Patty Jones, to the Bunch of Grapes in Third-street, near the second Presbyterian Church, shall receive Three Dollars and necessary expences, from Josiah F. Davenport. [*Pennsylvania Chronicle*, September 17, 1770]

[18] Stolen from the subscriber, on the 16th instant, by Elizabeth Dugal, who was hired in the house, the following things, viz. two chintz gowns, one dark, the other light, with sprigs and branches, and a coat of the same, one fine white callico gown, one blue India persian quilted coat, lined with light brown shalloon, almost new, one pair of stays, not half worn, one black peelong bonnet, trimmed with the same, three large silver spoons, marked A.M. and several other things, to the amount of 30 l. She carried with her, of her own, a blue durant or tammy gown, and pink calliman-co skirt, is about 27 years of age, of a fair complexion, pitted with the small pox, has a long nose, very thin hair, and of a middle stature; says she was born in Pennsylvania, where she may proba-bly be gone, though it is suspected she will make towards Carolina. Whoever will apprehend her, so that she may be brought to justice, shall have Two Pistoles reward. Lemuel Roberts. [Rind's *Virginia Gazette*, September 27, 1770]

[19] Five Pounds Reward. Run away the 13th of this instant September, from the subscribers, living in Leacock township, Lancaster county, a Negroe man and woman; the man is about 30 years old, 5 feet 4 inches high, speaks good English, has long hair; had on an old hat, his other clothes uncertain; — the woman who went with him, has with her a young female child, about 8 months old (a good mark to know them by) she is about 23 years old, middling size, had good clothes, two long gowns, one striped cotton, the other calicoe, two short gowns, and new low heeled shoes. Also a white servant man, named Adam Jacobs, who run away the 13th of June, is about 18 years of age, 5 feet 4 inches high, is somewhat marked with the small pox; had on, a white wool hat, a light coloured cloth jacket, with cuffs on the sleeves, old buckskin breeches; had also a pair of coarse linen trowsers, but what is most distinguishing, he has a large scar on his left leg, it having been run over by a waggon, also that knee is much larger than the other. Whoever secures them, so that their owner may get them again, shall receive the above reward, of Forty Shillings for the white man, Thirty for the Negroe man, and the same for the woman and child, paid by Samuel Lefever, or David Watson. [*Pennsylvania Gazette*, September 27, 1770]

[20] Ran away from me the Subscriber, an indented Negro Girl, about Eighteen or Nineteen Years of Age, middling Stature, with large Eyes, & goes by the name of Sarah Thompson, had on, when she went away, a Flannel Petticoat, and a short Gown, bare-footed and bare-legged. Whoever will take up said Girl, and secure her in any of his Majesty's Jails, or return her to me, shall have One Dollar Reward, and all necessary Charges paid, by Matthew Borden. N. B. Whoever entertains her shall suffer as the Law directs. It is imagined that he went to Providence where her Mother lives. [*Newport Mercury*, October 8, 1770]

[21] Absented herself from the Subscriber, on Thursday last, a tall stout Negro Wench, named Lucy, well known in and about Jacksonburgh; formerly the Property of Francis Oldfield, on Ponpon Neck. She had on when she went away a Callico Petticoat and Jacket: But as she took other Cloaths with her, may probably appear in other Dresses. Ten Pounds Currency Reward will be paid

to any Person who will give Information of her being harboured by a white Person, and One Dollar if by a Negro, on Conviction of the Offender; and Five Pounds like Money to any one who will deliver her to Mordecai Myers. [*South Carolina Gazette*, October 24, 1770]

[22] Run away from her master's service, yesterday morning, an English servant woman, named Margaret Stephens, aged about 19 years, middling sized, fair complexion, grey eyes, brown hair, hobbles in her gait, from a disorder she had on one of her ankles, has a remarkable scar on one of her hands, from a burn when a child, likewise a scar on each side of her eyes; took with her, one dark calicoe, and one light coloured camblet skirt, patched with dark patches, a broad striped lincey petticoat, an old blue and white striped quilted petticoat, very much patched, a white sarsnet bonnet, thread stockings, and calf skin shoes, four shifts, one of them ruffled, and several aprons, one of them check linen, another ozenbrigs. Whoever takes up the said servant, and secures her in any of his Majesty's goals, and gives notice thereof to her master, shall have Five Pounds reward, paid by me John Priestley. [*Pennsylvania Gazette*, November 1, 1770]

[23] Run away on Saturday morning October the 27th, 1770, from the subscriber, living in New-York, a negro wench named Lill, was born on Long-Island, and late the property of Mr. Jecamiah Mitchell, of Flushing, boatman. She is a tall thin wench, about seventeen years of age, rather upon the yellowish or tawny black, than otherwise; she had on when she went away, a thick coarse woollen jacket and petticoat, of an iron or russet colour; a blue cloth cloak with a hood to it, made of coarse knap; tho' she may change her dress, as she took with her a strip'd homespun jacket and petticoat, and sundry other things. Any person that secures the said wench, so that her master may have her again, shall have Twenty Shillings reward, and all reasonable charges paid; and all persons are hereby forewarned from harbouring or secreting the said wench, or detaining her from her said master, as they may depend upon being prosecuted to the utmost severity of the law, for so doing. Edward Agar. [*New York Gazette*, November 5, 1770]

[24] Committed to James City prison a Congo new Negro woman, named Betty, who cannot, or will not, tell her master's name; she is about 22 years old, is very big with child, and expect that she may lie in in about a month; she is about 4 feet high, has on an oznabrig shift and petticoat. The owner is desired to send for her, and pay charges to William S. Lane. [Rind's *Virginia Gazette*, November 15, 1770]

[25] Run away from the subscriber, an Irish servant woman, named Elizabeth Bryan, had on, when she went away, an old black quilted petticoat, old black cloak, calicoe short gown, striped silk handkerchief; she is about 35 years of age, 5 feet 4 inches high, a large scar on her right wrist, dark brown hair, and talks much with the brogue. Whoever secures said servant, so as her master may have her again, shall have Twenty Shillings reward, and reasonable charges, paid by Matthew Giffen. [*Pennsylvania Gazette*, November 15, 1770]

[26] Run away, on the 22d of November inst. from the Subscriber, living in Middletown, Bucks County, an Irish Servant Woman, named Anne McCarty, about 25 Years of Age, of a dark Complexion, dark brown Hair, small visage, and low thick Stature; had on, and took with her, a long stamped Linen Gown, a short Lincey Ditto, a Lincey Petticoat, striped cloak, blue and white, a Pair of wooden heeled Shoes, with Pinchbeck Buckles, not Fellows, and clouded Stockings; she speaks much with the Brogue, and it is thought is gone towards Philadelphia. Whoever takes up and secures said Servant, so as her master may have her again, shall have Forty Shillings Reward, and reasonable Charges, paid by David Marple. [*Pennsylvania Gazette*, November 29, 1770]

[27] Run away from the subscriber, on James river, about a month ago, a mulatto fellow named John Wilson, by trade a carpenter, 5 feet 9 or 10 inches high, 34 years of age, very well made sober and smooth in his discourse, has pretty long curling hair, which he generally wears tied behind, and has a mark on one of his shoulders of something resembling a shoulder of mutton. He has great variety of clothes, particularly a blue cloth coat and breeches, red cloth jacket, a pea jacket of black spotted cotton or flannel, brown

plains jacket, white linen and osnabrug shirts and trousers, and good shoes and stockings. He can read, write, and cipher very well, so that he is every way well qualified to attempt passing as a free-man, and, probably to get out of the country. All masters of vessels, and others, are therefore forewarned from employing, harbouring, or carrying said slave out of the colony. He has relations at my quarter in Bute county, North Carolina, and may steer that way southerly. I will give Forty Shillings to Whoever will deliver him to me, if taken in the country, and Ten Pounds if taken in any other province; Bute county, and about my quarter there, excepted. In that case, I will give Five Pounds. About a week after went off from the same place Sarah, a very lusty negro woman, about 19 years of age, very tall, and large footed, which she turns in pretty much. She is a very dark mulatto, with black freckles in her face, has a surly look, and is pretty saucy. She is sister to Wilson, and also has a good many clothes; but when she went away had on a dark coloured plains jacket and petticoat, with a border round the coat of red cloth like list. She had been run away for near a twelve-month before, and was taken up near Blandford and committed to Prince George prison, and had not been home above a fortnight before she went off again. It is very probable she is now in the neighbourhood of Blandford or Petersburg, as there are runaways always thereabouts. She pretends to pass for a freewoman. I will give Twenty Shillings to Whoever brings her home to me. William Black. [Purdie & Dixon's *Virginia Gazette*, December 13, 1770]

[28] Run away the 4th day of this instant December, from the subscriber, living in Brandywine Hundred, New Castle county, a servant girl, named Martha Eyers, about 22 years of age, fair hair; had on, when she went away, a brown bonnet, a blue cloak, and a white linen short gown, a striped linsey woolsey petticoat, and a pair of leather heeled shoes. It is thought she went to Philadelphia. Whoever takes up the said servant girl, and secures her, so that her master may have her again, shall have Ten Shillings reward, and reasonable charges, paid by Andrew McKee. [*Pennsylvania Gazette*, December 20, 1770]

1771

[29] Four Dollars Reward. Run away, the 9th of December, 1770, from the subscriber, living in Oxford township, Chester county, an Irish servant woman, named Mary Proctor, of a middle stature, about 25 years of age, black haired, talks a little on the brogue, is full of impudence, loves strong liquor, and will get drunk, when she has an opportunity; she is a good seamstress, and professes to be a mantua maker; had on, and took with her, an old blue bonnet, red silk handkerchief, redish calicoe gown, white linen apron, a mixed lincey petticoat, a plad ditto, and flat heeled shoes; she says she was born in the city of Cork, in Ireland, and came from thence about a year or two ago, but it is supposed she has been longer in this country; she has been acquainted with both Workhouse and Barracks in Philadelphia, and is of a very ordinary conduct. Whoever takes up said servant, and secures her, so that I may have her again, shall have the above reward, and reasonable charges, paid by me William Sterritt.

N. B. She may change her name, and also her clothes. [*Pennsylvania Gazette,* January 3, 1771]

[30] Ran away, the 17th of November last, from the subscriber, a Dutch servant girl, named Elizabeth Eckrine, a thick clumsy ill-tongued slut, full faced, brown hair. Had, and took with her, two short gowns, one callico, the other striped, a cross-barred, and two striped flannel petticoats, a Leghorn hat, a pair of wax leather shoes. Whoever takes up the said servant, and brings her to her

master, shall receive Six Pence reward. Richard Martin. [*Pennsylvania Chronicle*, January 7, 1771]

[31] Run away from the Subscriber, the 27th of May last, a Negro Wench named Hannah, twenty-eight Years old, about five Feet five Inches high, well made, has a down look, speaks short and surly, and the Whites of her Eyes remarkably red; had on when she went away a black Yarn Serge Jacket and white Yarn Serge Petticoat, Osnabrug Shift, and carried with her some other Clothes. She is supposed to be lurking about Mr. John Mason's Quarters, on Meherrin River, Southampton County, where she has some Relations. Whoever will apprehend the said Wench, and bring her to me, shall have Forty Shillings Reward; and if taken out of this Colony, Five Pounds. John Thweat.

N. B. As she has a Notion of Freedom, she may perhaps pass as a free Wench, where she is not known. [Purdie & Dixon's *Virginia Gazette*, January 10, 1771]

[32] On the 29th day of October last, came to the subscriber's house, in Charlestown township, Chester county, a certain woman, who called herself Margaret Spicer, being her maiden name, and said she was married to one Samuel White, and lodged there over night, with her female child, about 9 or 10 months old; and next day went off, and left the said child at the subscriber, and never returned again; she wore an old green whalebone bonnet, a short linen bedgown, striped blue and white, linsey petticoat, striped blue and white, white yarn stockings, and old calfskin shoes; all her apparel very mean, and ragged; she has reddish hair and freckled face, is of a middle stature, hath a little of the brogue on her tongue, and smoaks tobacco. Whoever takes up the said Margaret Spicer, alias White, and brings her to the subscriber, shall receive Twenty Shillings reward, and reasonable charges. Griffith Jones. [*Pennsylvania Gazette*, January 17, 1771]

[33] Eight Dollars Reward. Run away from the subscriber last Sunday morning, an indented servant man named James Samuel Gordon, about 26 years of age, born in London, but possibly may change his name, by trade a jeweler, a diminutive fellow, about 5 feet 1 inch high, black hair tied behind, thin vissage, pale faced,

and speaks the French language, and is much given to lying: Had on when he went away, a blossom colour'd coat and breeches, superfine cloth; red jacket, white cotton stockings, and pinchbeck buckles, with beaver hat, &c. Took sundry other cloaths, likewise a parcel of jeweller's tools, which he stole away with him; is suppos'd to be in company with a woman which he calls his wife, Mary Gordon, alias Mary Dill, about five feet four inches high, pale fac'd, down look, takes snuff and much addicted to drink, and a great lyar: Had on when she went away, either a bloom colour'd poplin, or cotton gown, blue worsted stockings, black stuff shoes, and white bonnet. Whoever takes up and secures said servant, so that his master may have him again, shall receive the above reward, and reasonable charges, paid by the subscriber, living in Second street, Philadelphia. Edmond Milne, Goldsmith. [New York Gazette, April 8, 1771]

[34] Forty Shillings Reward. Ran away, from the subscriber, living in Northampton county, New Jersey, between Mount Holly and Burlington, one John Alcut, a flatman, about 5 feet 10 inches high, a very likely portly looking man. Had on a grey bearskin surtout coat, a pair of leather breeches, and a good beaver hat. Went off with him, one Margaret Elton, the wife of Thomas Elton, a very likely round-favoured woman. She had on a black crape gown. They are supposed to be gone to Baltimore in Maryland. Whoever will apprehend and secure the said Alcut, in any of his Majesty's gaols, so that I may obtain Justice, shall have the above reward, paid by Ruel Elton.

    N. B. Said Alcut, carried three flat loads of wood to Philadelphia, sold it, and is gone off with the Money. [Pennsylvania Chronicle, April 22, 1771]

[35] Fourteen Dollars Reward. Run away from the subscribers, living in Philadelphia, on the 13th of April last, the following servants, viz. Two servant men, Taylors by trade, one named John Christie, a short thick fellow, calls himself a Scotchman, about 26 years of age, remarkably thick legs, has lightish coloured hair, cut short, walks pretty much upon his heels; had on, when he went away, a pair of old shoes and odd buckles, old white thread ribbed stockings, a snuff or rather a yellowish coarse cloth coat, with plain

round gilt buttons, black jacket and breeches, one white and one check shirt, an old coarse hat, and has a sort of a scar round one of his eyes, which he got by fighting, he is very talkative, more especially when in liquor, and speaks pretty broad. The other, named John Black, a very simple fellow, about 23 years of age, and about half a head taller than Christie, a Scotchman, he is pretty hard of hearing, speaks but little and low, as the hard hearing people generally do when they speak, he is a thick fellow, very thick legs, round breast, and sticks out pretty much, full faced, dark hair, cut short; had on, when he went away, a pair of old shoes, blue breeches, red jacket, a coarse claret coloured cloth coat, with a small cape, turned down, the pockets in the side plaits, with 3 buttons in each, and an old coarse hat. The other is a Welsh servant girl, named Anne Edmund, who was inticed away by the said John Christie, as he used to be continually after her, and they would meet and get together as often as they possibly could, and no doubt she will pass for said Christie's wife; she is about 19 years of age, middling size, broad smooth face, fresh complexion, short nose, black eyes, her fore teeth very white, and pretty wide apart from each other, has blackish hair, pretty curly before, speaks bad English, walks quick and heavy, very talkative, and very apt to tell lies; she came from Bristol, in the ship Chalkley, Captain Peter Young, about 12 months ago; she had on, and took with her, when she went away, two calicoe gowns, one dark, the other a purple in diamonds, much worn, also a short striped linen ditto, 1 white and some check aprons, 2 shifts, one of hemp linen, the other about half worn, new leather shoes, with large round white metal buckles, old blue worsted stockings, a short red cloak, with a hood to it, a chip hat, with a blue and white ribbon on. Said Christie has lived in Maryland, and came from there, and supposed he was a convict, as he never would tell where he came from; he knows a great many people in or about Baltimore: It is probable they may change their names and clothes. Whoever takes up said servants, and secures them in any goal, or brings them back, so that their masters may have them again, shall have Forty Shillings for each man, and Twenty-five Shillings for the girl, reward, and all reasonable charges, paid by us John Reedle, Christopher Pechin. [*Pennsylvania Gazette*, May 16, 1771]

{36} Run away from the Subscriber, in Bedford County, on Great Falling River, an Irish Servant Man named Michael Kelly, about five Feet five Inches high, with short black Hair, wears a cut brown Wig, a blue Broadcloth Coat, spotted Flannel Jacket, and a Pair of old patched Breeches. Also an Irish Servant Woman named Margaret Kelly, Wife to the said Michael. She wore a blue Calimanco Gown and Petticoat. They both speak Irish; but neither of them are known to speak English. I will give Five Pounds Reward on their being delivered to me, and Fifty Shillings, if they are secured in any Jail in this Colony, upon Information of the same given to William Hayth. [Purdie & Dixon's *Virginia Gazette*, May 16, 1771]

{37} Run away, in the evening of the 25th instant, from James Reynolds, Carver and Gilder, in Front street, Philadelphia, an indented servant girl, named Mary Hadley, came from Roxiter, in the county of Salop, in Old England, and was purchased but two days before from on board the Betsey, Captain Hood, from Bristol; she is a good looking country girl, about 5 feet 4 inches high, ruddy complexion, and stout built; had on a striped brown stuff gown, pretty much worn, black petticoat, check apron, and wore a black sattin bonnet, with a puckered caul. It is pretty certain she went off with a man, who said he was her first cousin, and called himself John Hadley, came over a redemptioner in the above ship, a husbandman by profession, but appears more like a seaman, being dressed in a brown jacket, black waistcoat, and long oznabrig trowsers; about 5 feet 7 inches high, down look, and wears his own brown hair. Whoever secures said persons, or either of them, in any of his Majesty's goals, either in Pennsylvania or the Jerseys, so that their masters may have them again, shall receive Three Dollars for each, and reasonable charges, from the aforesaid James Reynolds, and Seymour Hood. [*Pennsylvania Chronicle*, May 27, 1771]

{38} Run away from the subscriber hereto, the evening following the 12th of May last past from Milford, in the colony of Connecticut, in New England, a negro man named Newport, aged 29 years, a stout, well set, broad shoulder'd fellow, for height about middling, rather stoops when walking, if carefully observed, was born in Newport, Rhode Island, talks plain. He carried with him, one brown homespun flannel coat and breeches almost new, and one scarlet broad cloth vest, with flowered pewter buttons, also one coarse cinamon colour'd lappel'd broad cloth coat with metal buttons, one blue and one white striped lappel'd linen vest, one such shirt, one fine white ditto. three coarse check'd woolen ditto, one course flannel outside jacket, and great coat mix'd black and white wool, two pair ribb'd stockings, one pale blue worsted, the other brown thread, one old beaver hat, with a white metal button, and silver'd loop. The same night went from the same house, a large white feemale, aged about 27 years, red hair, stoops as she walks about her housework. Carried off with her sundry aprons, some blue and white small check linen, and some white, one scarlet broad cloth short cloak, much worn with a silver lace about the same, and a woman's black sattin bonnet almost new. She had of her own with her, sundry new tow cloth smocks, several petticoats, striped new linen blue and white short gown, some blue and white check woolen aprons, two check linen handkerchiefs, is something near sighted, wore men's shoes. They were seen about 14 miles to the northward. Whoever will take up said negro, and convey him to the subscriber, or secure him so that he gets him again, if taken in this colony shall receive Five Dollars, if out of this colony Eight Dollars reward and all necessary charges – and if any of the articles supposed stolen by the feemale be taken and return'd, the person that returns them shall receive half the value of what may be so returned. The foregoing reward shall be paid by Edward Allen.

N. B. If said negro hears of this advertisement and shall return to his duty within one month from the date, he shall be received into his master's service, without corporal punishment. [*Connecticut Courant*, July 9, 1771]

[39] Run away, yesterday, from the Subscriber, living near Gunpowder Falls, 9 miles from Baltimore-town, a convict servant woman named Sarah Hill, about 22 years of age, of a middling size, grey eyes and short yellow hair, she has a boil on one of her arms. Had on when she went away, a black bonnet, a red handker-

chief bird's eyed, a blue calimanco gown almost new, a black quilted petticoat with large diamonds; she had neither shoes nor stockings; she is fresh-coloured, and has one or two large marks near her
mouth from the small-pox.

Whoever takes up said woman, and secures her, so that her
Master may get her again, shall have Four Pounds reward, and rea-
sonable charges if brought home, paid by John Christopher.
[*Pennsylvania Chronicle*, September 2, 1771]

[40] Ran away, last Saturday evening, from the Subscriber, an Irish
servant Girl, named Rachel Harding, about 17 years of age, of a
middle stature, and marked with the small-pox. Had on, when she
went away, a striped short gown, blue stuff petticoat, &c. Whoever
takes her up, and brings her to me, shall have Six Pence reward.
Francis Harris. [*Pennsylvania Chronicle*, September 2, 1771]

[41] Committed to the gaol of Elizabeth City county, on Monday
the 26th of this instant, a small outlandish Negro woman; her
cloathing is an oznabrigs shift and petticoat, and Virginia cloth
waistcoat. She speaks little or no English. All that I can learn from
her is, that she belongs to one Mr. Ruff, who lives in a great town,
by a grandy water. She appears to be in the 6th or 7th month of
her pregnancy. The owner is desired to come or send for her, as
soon as possible, as the state of her condition will make her very
expensive to Edward Hurst, gaoler. [Rind's *Virginia Gazette*,
September 5, 1771]

[42] Run away from the Subscriber, near Petersburg, the 18th of
last May, two new Negroes, namely, a Fellow named Step, about
six Feet high, has his Country Marks on his Temples, and has lost
some of his fore Teeth. He appears to have a very honest
Countenance, and is supposed to be about twenty Years of Age; he
had with him, when he went away, a white Plains Waistcoat and
Breeches, Osnabrug Shirt, and a tolerable good bound Hat. The
other a Girl named Lucy, supposed to be about twelve Years of
Age, and had on a white Plains Petticoat and striped Virginia
Cloth Waistcoat. Neither of them can speak good English, as they
have not been long in the Country. They went off with several others, being persuaded that they could find the Way back to their

own Country. They were discovered, about six Weeks after their going off, near Blanton's Ferry, in Mecklenburg County, where the Gang was dispersed, and three of them taken, one of whom belonged to me. The said negroes are outlawed. Five Pounds for each will be given if taken within this Colony, and Ten Pounds for each if in any other. George Robertson. [Purdie & Dixon's *Virginia Gazette,* September 12, 1771]

[43] Ran away on Saturday the 12th instant, from the subscriber, living at the Ship-yards, an indented servant girl, named Catherine Beasley, about 15 years of age, fair complexion, smooth faced, of a middling stature, blue ey'd; had on a callico gown, blue quilted petticoat, and took with her several other clothes. Whoever takes up and returns the said servant girl, to me the subscriber, shall be handsomely rewarded for their trouble, and any person, who keeps, or entertains her, shall be prosecuted as the law directs, by James Dickson. [*New York Journal*, October 17, 1771]

[44] Run away on Monday the 14th Instant, from the Subscriber, living in Irish-Street, a High Dutch Servant Girl named Catharine Araway Gustan, about 16 Years of Age, short and well made, brown Hair, and is pretty much marked with the Small-Pox: Had on when she went away, a black and white Stuft Petty-coat, and a red and white do, rather long for her, an Ozenbrigs short Gown, a short red Cloak, a black Bonnet, and Shoes and Stockings. She ran away once before, and was harboured at Jamaica, on Long Island. Whoever takes up the said Runaway, so that her Master may have her again shall receive 20s. if taken in the City, and 3 Dollars if out of the same, paid by George Campbell. [*New York Gazette*, October 21, 1771]

[45] Run away from the Subscriber, in April last, dark Mulatto Woman named Hankey, alias Hagai Sexton, between two and three and twenty Years of Age, about five Feet high, has long black curled Hair tied behind, remarkable bow Legs, and is very talkative; she had on, when she went away, a cross barred Pompadour Ground Stuff Gown, an Osnabrug Shift and Petticoat, and an old dressed Gauze Cap. She was born in Caroline County, is well known about Port Royal, at which Place she has several Times

been seen since her Elopement, and in July last was entertained at the Plantation of Mr. John Macon in that County, but has since left that Place, and is supposed to be gone towards Williamsburg. [Purdie & Dixon's *Virginia Gazette,* October 31, 1771]

[46] Run away from Williamsburg, last Week, a tall slim Negro Woman named Rachel, clothed in green Half-thicks, which Dress she may have changed, has a Scar on one of her Eyes, and is big with Child. Whoever will deliver her to the Subscriber, at York, or secures her so that she may be had again, shall have Twenty Shillings Reward. Allen Jones. [Purdie & Dixon's *Virginia Gazette*, November 14, 1771]

[47] Run away from the subscriber, in New York, on Monday the 26th of October, and was seen at King's Bridge on Wednesday the 28th, an Irish servant girl, named Elizabeth Currie, about eighteen years old, of a fair complexion, freckled, smooth faced, light brown hair, not above two or three inches long; had on a broad blue and white striped homespun petticoat, and a smaller striped blue and white jacket, no cap on, an old round black hat, no ribband to the crown, a course dowlas apron; was bare footed, had no shoes, smooth tongued, and a very great liar; was seen to pass the old bridge in the above dress, in company with a man in a red or reddish coat or waistcoat; she had no other clothes with her, and cannot easily alter her dress; is supposed to have gone the Albany road. Any person that will secure the said runaway, shall have Two Pounds reward, and Twenty Shillings if they can secure the fellow that carried her off, so that he can be brought to justice, and all reasonable charges paid them. All masters of vessels are forbid harbouring or carrying her off as they will answer the same to Alexander Leslie. [*New York Journal*, November 19, 1771]

1772

[48] There are two old Negroes lurking about my Plantation, one a Man, named Cuffy, the other a Woman, named Grace; they are outlandish Negroes, and speak very bad, although they have been in the Country a Number of Years; they are cloathed in Negro Cotton; the Man is bald, and has a remarkable large Navel. The Owner is desired to come and take them away. Francis Peters. [Purdie & Dixon's *Virginia Gazette,* March 12, 1772]

[49] Six Dollars Reward. Run away on the 18th of October, 1771, at night, from the subscriber, living at the Sign of the Bible-in-Heart, in Strawberry alley, an indented servant woman, named Eleanor Armstrong, about 5 feet 4 inches high, pretty lusty, brown complexion, large featured, dark sooty coloured hair, about 26 years of age, has a large mouth, and an excellent sett of teeth; she takes snuff immoderately at the right side of her nose, says she was born near the city of Armagh, in Ireland, and came to this city in the Newry Packet, Captain Robinson, in June last; had on, and took with her, when she went away, a long chints wrapper, of a yellow ground, with large red and brown sunflowers the pattern, the sleeves pieced near the cuff, with red and brown spotted calicoe, and broke under the arms; and over said wrapper, a short gown, with some red and white stripes and sprigs through it, a good deal worn, and pieced under the arms with check linen, the colour much faded; a new camblet skirt, of a deep blue, and one old ditto, of a light blue colour, a good small check apron, of a bad colour, a

green Barcelona handkerchief, much faded, one large blue and white check ditto, marked in one corner E.E. a clean cap, with a black sattin ribbon, tied round her head, and brought under her chin, a blue cloth cloak, with a cap to it, tied at the neck with a narrow worsted tape; an old changeable silk bonnet, lined with blue silk, and tied with a white ribbon; 3 coarse shifts, one of which is a homespun, with a pair of fine sleeves, one ozenbrigs ditto, and one coarse tow ditto, with broken ruffles on the same; a pair of blue yarn stockings, a pair of coarse white ditto, a pair of mens shoes, half soaled, with one brass buckle, and one steel ditto, pierced in the rim; she wore on the middle finger of her right hand a brass ring, is much given to liquor, and when in liquor, is apt to laugh greatly, speaks with the Irish tone. As she takes delight in no other work than spinning, it is thought she has hired herself some where in the country for that purpose; and, as she hath been gone so long, it is probable she has changed her dress; she will be apt to alter her name to Fulton; she was seen in Burlington a few weeks ago, in company with another woman. All masters of vessels and others, are forbid to harbour or carry her off, as they may depend upon being proceeded against, as the law directs. Whoever takes up and secures said servant, so that her master may have her again, shall receive the above reward, with reasonable charges, paid by William Evitt. [*Pennsylvania Gazette*, April 2, 1772]

[50] Ran away, from the subscriber, a Scotch servant woman, named Ann M'Daniel, about 40 years of age, speaks much in the Scotch dialect, has red hair, and is pock-marked. Had on, when she went away, a check gown, with broad stripes, stripe linsey petticoat, and a blue linsey bed gown, with some other clothes, not known what sort. She is a good spinner, of wool or flax, and it is thought will go about either begging or spinning. She took with her a child about three years of age, speaks much in the same dialect. Whoever takes up said woman, and secures her, so that her master may have her again, shall receive the reward of Twenty Shillings, and reasonable charges, if brought home, paid by James Holliday, shoemaker.

N. B. As she is an old offender, it is hoped that any honest person knowing her will take her up. [*Pennsylvania Chronicle*, June 8, 1772]

[51] Ran away, from the subscriber, on Tuesday evening the 19th of May, an indented servant woman, named Ann Wasson, much marked with the small-pox, has a hole or dent in one of her wrists, is a tall lusty woman, had on when she went away, a blue and white linsey petticoat, blue and white figured callico gown, a pair of leather pumps; has a hole or dent in her nose, and is newly come from Ireland. Whoever takes up and secures said servant, so that her master may get her again, shall have Thirty Shillings reward, paid by Thomas Cooch, jun. (living near Christiana Bridge.) [*Pennsylvania Chronicle*, June 8, 1772]

[52] Committed to James City Prison, on Saturday the 11th Instant (July) a Negro Woman who says her Name is Molly, and that she is the Property of the Honourable William Byrd; she is of a yellow Complexion, about forty Years of Age, of the middle Stature, well made, has on an Osnabrug Waistcoat, Coat, Shift, and Petticoat, and a Virginia Yarn Ditto, with white Warping and blue Filling. The Owner is desired to take her away, and pay the necessary Charges. John Connally, Jailer. [Purdie & Dixon's *Virginia Gazette*, July 16, 1772]

[53] Run away, the 13th of this instant July, from the subscriber, near Newtown, Bucks County, an Irish servant girl, named Judy Fagan, between 15 and 16 years old, of a dark completion, has black hair and grey eyes; had on when she went away, a long old green worsted gown, brown skirt and black bonnet, no shoes nor stockings. Whoever takes up and secures said girl, so that her master may have her again, shall have twenty shillings reward and reasonable charges paid by Thomas Morgan. [*Pennsylvania Gazette*, July 23, 1772]

[54] Ran away, on Sunday the 19th instant, from the subscriber, at Newport, an Irish indented maid servant, named Elioner Clievland, pretty tall, who is very corpulent, with a red complexion, brown hair, and has a scar and large dent in one of her arms, had on a red pompadore gown, and light broad cloth cloak. Whoever will apprehend said servant, and return her to the subscriber, or confine her in one of his Majesty's gaols, and give notice thereof, shall have four Dollars reward, and all necessary charges, paid by John Warren. [*Newport Mercury*, July 27, 1772]

[55] Five Dollars Reward. Run away from the subscriber, near the New Dutch church, New York, two Irish servant women, the one named Ann Miller, of a swarthy complexion, black hair, and a black beard on her upper lip, about twenty five or thirty years old: had on when she went away, a black petticoat, and a flowered linen bed gown, with the flowers wash'd almost white, a white linen handkerchief about her neck, and took with her a blue and white small striped linen gown, a blue and white broad striped home-spun petticoat, blue worsted stockings, and old leather shoes. The other Elizabeth Curry, about eighteen years old, of a fair complexion, freckled in the face, fair hair, had on a broad blue and white homespun petticoat, and a cotton bed gown, of a red ground, a diamond figure, a dark checkered silk handkerchief about her neck, no cloak, hat, or cap on her head; and took with her a common India linen gown, black and redish brown spotted figure with small check aprons each, leather shoes and some other things. 'Tis supposed they went off with Mr. Henry Usticks two nailers, that went off the same time towards Kingsbridge, or the iron works in the Jerseys. Any person that will apprehend the said runaways, shall have the above reward, and all reasonable charges paid them; and all persons are forewarned not to harbour or conceal them, or any master of vessels to carry them off, at their peril. Alexander Leslie. [New York Journal, July 30, 1772]

[56] Forty Shillings Reward. Run away, the 1st of this instant August, from the subscriber, living in Salisbury township, Lancaster county, a servant girl, named Catherine McDaniel; had on, and took with her, a linen check bonnet, and white linen bed gown a brown lincey ditto, two petticoats, one brown lincey, the same of the bed gown, the other tow linen, 2 coarse shifts, 2 or 3 tow aprons, a red cloak, and small check handkerchief, no shoes, nor stockings; she has a bold look, is about 5 feet 1 or 2 inches high, has brown hair, full faced, full brown eyes, very talkative, and lived some time in the city of Philadelphia, with Mr. William Graham, at the Sign of the Black Horse. Whoever takes up said servant, and confines her in any goal, shall have the above reward, and if brought home, reasonable charges, paid by Henry Cowen. [Pennsylvania Gazette, August 12, 1772]

[57] Run away from the subscriber in Leesburg, the 4th instant, a servant woman named Elizabeth Smith, 25 years old, about 5 feet 4 or 5 inches high, her hair very black, has several scars on her under lip, chin, and arms, and much pitted with the smallpox; had on, and took with her, a short black calico gown, a white linen ditto, white apron, and white humhum sack and petticoat, red cardinal, flowered blue sattin capuchin, calico petticoat, black sattin laced bonnet, one pair of cotton and two pair of hose, old black calimanco shoes with plain silver buckles, one ruffled and two plain shifts. It is probable she may have taken many other things that are not missed. She was formerly indented to Capt. Gray, from Boston, and may now perhaps have an old indenture. Whoever takes up the said servant, and brings her to me, shall have Five Pounds, besides what the law allows. Alexander M'intyre. [Rind's *Virginia Gazette*, October 22, 1772]

[58] Run away from the subscriber, near Facer courthouse, on Sunday the 4th of October, a Negro Woman named Milla, of a yellow complexion, short and likely; had on a short striped Virginia cloth gown and petticoat, oznabrig shift and bonnet. I understand she endeavours to pass for a free woman. Whoever apprehends the said Negro so that I may get her, shall be well rewarded, by John Hudnall. [Rind's *Virginia Gazette*, November 19, 1772]

[59] Run away from the Subscriber, in New Kent, a Virginia born Negro Woman named Betty, about twenty seven Years old, of a middle Stature, and has a Scar on her Breast occasioned by a Stroke from her Overseer; her Clothing Virginia Cloth, but probably may change her Dress. She is supposed to be lurking about Williamsburg. Whoever conveys the said Slave to me shall have Forty Shillings Reward, and Thirty Shillings to secure her so that I get her again. Francis Tyree, Senior. [Purdie & Dixon's *Virginia Gazette*, December 3, 1772]

1773

[60] Run away from the subscriber, on the 25th of December last, a Negro Wench, named Philis, late the property of William Smith, Esq; She had on when she went away, a light coloured calimanco gown, a check apron, black silk cloak, and a black peelong bonnet. Said Wench is marked in the forehead with a diamond, has lost several of her fingers on each hand, and also some of her toes. Whoever takes up and secures said Wench, so that she may be had again, shall receive Twenty Shillings reward, and all reasonable charges, paid by Mary Exceen. [*New York Gazette*, January 4, 1773]

[61] Ran away from the subscriber in Newport, on the night of the 1st instant, an indented Irish maid servant, about 28 years of age; she is pretty short and thick, of a very red complexion, and is supposed to have had on a red short cloak, a black bonnet, a green camblet gown, a brown camblet skirt, a checked apron, and carried away a bundle of other clothes. Whoever will apprehend said runaway and return her home, or secure her in any of his Majesty's jails, and give notice thereof, shall be handsomely rewarded by George Nichols. [*Newport Mercury*, January 4, 1773]

[62] Run away from the subscriber, living in Philadelphia, a negroe woman named Phoebe; she is a short woman, and has a scar on her right eye-brow; had on, when she went away, a striped lincey jacket, and black quilted petticoat; has with her a female Negroe child, about two years old; she is thought to be gone

towards Bordentown. Whoever takes up said Negroe, and secures her in any goal, so as her master may get her again, shall have Twenty-Shillings reward, and all reasonable charges, paid by John Hazelwood. [*Pennsylvania Gazette*, January 6, 1773]

[63] Eight Dollars Reward. Run Away, on the 6th instant, from the subscriber, living in Second street, Philadelphia, a Dutch servant woman, named Elizabeth Bone, about 21 years of age, well built, light hair, fair complexion, broad smooth face, short nose, fresh colour, and a good sett of teeth; had on an English cap, with a coarse lawn border, check cotton handkerchief, a new striped lincey jacket, an old Dutch lincey petticoat, a homespun tow apron, coarse blue stockings, with white clocks, mens shoes, with small carved buckles; she took with her one linen cap, one check cotton handkerchief, one tow apron, checked with blue wool. Whoever takes her up, and brings her home, or secures her in any goal in this province, so that her master may have her again, shall have the above reward, and reasonable charges, paid by Abraham Wayne. [*Pennsylvania Gazette*, January 13, 1773]

[64] Ran away from the Subscriber a Negro Girl named Dinah, aged about 20 Years, of a yellow Complection, with a cast in one of her Eyes. She had on when she went away, an old yellowish Riding hood, two homespun Petticoats, and a homespun short Gown with Leather Buttons. She formerly belonged to Mr. Maxwell, in King street. Whoever shall take her up and deliver her to her Master, shall be handsomely rewarded, and have all necessary Charges paid by John Deselver. [*Boston Post Boy*, January 18, 1773]

[65] Run away from the Subscriber, in King William, a middle aged Convict Servant Woman named Mary Davis, stout made, with a swarthy Complexion, much pitted with the Smallpox, has black Hair, always talks as if she had a bad Cold, and it is supposed will change her Name; she had on a dark Camlet Gown, a black Hat, and a red Silk Handkerchief about her Neck. It is probable she will make towards Rappahannock, as she was often inquiring whether many vessels lay there. I will give Twenty Shillings Reward to any Person that will secure her so that I may get her

again. John Catlett. [Purdie & Dixon's *Virginia Gazette*, January 21, 1773]

[66] Run away, on the 27th day of last month, from the subscriber, living in Newtown township, and county aforesaid, a Dutch servant girl, named Carolina de Pool, aged about 23 years, came from Rotterdam last fall; she is a short chunky body, one shoulder is a little higher than the other, hath light coloured hair, a large humped nose, and a hardy bold look; had on, when she went away, a round ear'd cap, blue stamped handkerchief, and new dark coloured short gown, an old Dutch upper petticoat, striped, of a dirty colour, blue stockings, English shoes, and carved buckles in them. Whoever takes up said servant, and brings her home to her master, shall have Thirty-shillings reward, and reasonable charges, paid by Joseph Kaighin. [*Pennsylvania Gazette*, February 10, 1773]

[67] Twenty Shillings Reward. Run Away, the second of this instant February, from the subscriber, in St. George's Hundred, New castle county, an Irish servant girl, named Betty Slone, but calls herself Kitty Owen, about 20 years of age, a middle sized woman, with fair hair, fresh complexion, light blue eyes, thin lips, pitted with the smallpox, her hair is very thin, by a spell of sickness that she had, and cut short before, a great singer and talker, and is fond of men; had on, and took with her, when she went away, a black and white linsey petticoat, black quilt, a flannel ditto, a black and white short gown, a purple and white calicoe gown, with ruffles at the sleeves, a dark calicoe short ditto, two 800 shifts, a tow apron, one striped ditto, blue yarn stockings, two pair of shoes, one pair with leather heels, split at the instep and a piece set in, carved metal buckles, a chip hat, with a red ribbon round the crown of it. Whoever takes up said servant, and secures her in any of his Majesty goals, so that her master may have her again, shall have the above reward, and reasonable charges, paid by William Read. [*Pennsylvania Gazette*, February 17, 1773]

[68] A Quarter of a Dollar Reward. Run away in the night between the 3d and 4th of this inst. February from the subscriber, living in Germantown, a German servant girl, named Elizabeth Prugelin, of a melancholy temper, red eyes, and speaks Low Dutch

and French, is about 26 years old; had on when she went away, a new lincey red, blue and white striped jacket, and white, dark and light-blue striped petticoat, new fulled stockings, and almost new shoes. Whoever takes up said servant girl, and brings her to her master, shall have the above reward, paid by Christopher Sower, Printer.

N. B. Any person knowing where she is, and inclining to buy her time of servitude, it being three years and four months, may have her very cheap. [*Pennsylvania Packet*, February 22, 1773]

[69] Three Pounds Reward. Run away from the subscriber, living near Canawingo Creek, Little Britain Township, Lancaster County, on Friday, the 15th of January, a Mulattoe woman, about 18 or 19 years of age, she calls herself Hannah Cambel, is a bold well tongued hussy, of a whitish cast, very much freckled in the face, has a brown spot on one of her little fingers, and commonly wears her hair tied; had on, when she went away, a light coloured lincey jacket and petticoat, and it is supposed she had other clothes, she wore white stockings, with blue clocks, high heeled shoes, and it is thought she will dress herself in mens clothes. Whoever takes up said wench, and brings her home to her master, or secures her in any of his Majesty's goals, so as he may get her again, shall have the above reward, and reasonable charges, paid by Moses Davison. [*Pennsylvania Gazette*, February 24, 1773]

[70] Run away, last Night, from the Subscriber, two Slaves, namely: A Negro Fellow named Fortune, about six Feet high, slim made, has a thin Nose for one so black as he is, and appears to be about forty Years of Age; he took with him sundry Wearing Apparel, particularly a Pair of Buckskin Breeches almost new, a Thickset Coat, a brown Sailor's Jacket, a red great Coat, a fine Hat, pretty much worn, with a large Brim, and commonly has it cocked up, wears a red Worsted Cap in common, and sometimes a Silk one. Also a Wench named Aminta, appears to be about thirty Years of Age, short and well made, has much the Look of an Indian, and is so, her Mother having been brought from the Spanish Main to Rhode Island, has long black Hair, which she wears in her Neck, and took with her a black Quilt, a red Flannel

Petticoat, a dark Ground Calico Gown, a blue and white one, and an old light coloured Stuff ditto, a red Cardinal, a black Bonnet, and several other Things. I lately had them of Captain John Atkinson, and as they were brought from Rhode Island, it is probable they will endeavour to get there again, as they pretend to Freedom. I request it as a Favour of all Masters of Vessels not to harbour or entertain them, as it will probably be attended with bad Consequences. I will give a Reward of Three Pounds if they are taken fifty Miles from home and secured so that I may get them again, and Thirty Shillings if within that Distance. William Bradley. [Purdie & Dixon's *Virginia Gazette*, April 29, 1773]

[71] Run away from the Subscriber, in King and Queen, about the Middle of March last, a Country born Negro Woman named Sarah, a very lusty stout made Wench, about two and twenty Years of age, very artful, and, though not a Mulatto, may attempt to pass for a free Woman. She carried with her several Changes of Apparel, among which are remembered a red and white Calico Jacket and Petticoat, a white Holland and blue Plains Ditto, a red Flannel Petticoat, a purple Cloth Cloak, a black furred Hat, with a Gold Band, Button, and Loop, a black Silk Hat, several white Linen Shifts and Aprons, a spotted Yarn Rug and Dutch Blanket, a Pair of English made Leather Shoes, and several Pairs of Thread, Cotton, and Worsted Stockings, with a small red Leather Trunk. She has been chiefly a House Servant, is a fine Sempstress, Knitter, Washer, and Ironer, was born, and chiefly lived, on James River, in Prince George County, and is supposed to be lurking somewhere near Maycox, Merchant's Hope, or up about Petersburg. If she is apprehended on the south side of James River I will give Forty Shillings Reward with reasonable travelling Charges for bringing her to me; and if nearer, Twenty Shillings. William Black. [Purdie & Dixon's *Virginia Gazette*, May 6, 1773]

[72] Run away from Roslin, in Chesterfield, about the 26th of April last, two New Negroes, one of them a small black Fellow, about thirty Years of Age, the other a middle sized Wench, about twenty seven Years old, both clothed in white Cotton and Plaid Hose; the Wench carried with her a Pair of new Leather Shoes,

with wooden Heels. Whoever brings them to me, or to Mr. Russell, at Blandford, shall receive a handsome Reward. Charles Duncan. [Purdie & Dixon's *Virginia Gazette*, May 6, 1773]

[73] Run away from the Subscriber, on Whiteoak Swamp, in Henrico, about the last of January, a likely Negro Wench named Sall, about twenty Years old, very black, short, and well proportioned; her Dress was of the common Kind wore by Plantation Negroes, but has a Variety of fine Clothes. She has been seen about Richmond and Warwick, on James River. All Masters of Vessels are cautioned against harbouring or carrying her out of the Colony. Whoever delivers her to me shall have Forty Shillings if she is taken in the Colony, and Five Pounds if out thereof, besides the Allowance by Law. William Ferris, Junior. [Purdie & Dixon's *Virginia Gazette*, May 6, 1773]

[74] Ran away, last Friday night, from the Subscriber, a servant woman, named Mary Wilkins, lately imported in the snow Restoration, Capt. James Thomas, from Bristol; she is a lusty well looking young woman, remarkably fresh coloured, and speaks quick and bold; she carried off many clothes of her own, besides robbing her master of several things of value. At the same time, ran away, from the above mentioned vessel, two sailors, who are supposed to have assisted her in robbing her master, and are gone off with her. One an Irishman, named Nathaniel Maddin, about 5 feet 8 inches high, of a ruddy complexion, has black hair, and a cast in one of his eyes; he wore a blue upper jacket, and a red and white stip'd waistcoat. The other an Englishman, named George Robinson, about 5 feet 7 inches high, of a ruddy complexion, has black curled hair, and dressed in seaman's clothes. Whoever takes up this said servant woman, and secures her, so that her master may have her again, shall receive Five Pounds reward, and the like sum for each of the said men, if taken up and convicted of the Robbery to be paid by James Chambers. [*New York Journal*, May 13, 1773]

[75] Ran away the 21st of this instant from the subscriber, living near Gunpowder meetinghouse, in Baltimore County, a mulatto woman named Margaret Grant, about twenty years old; she is very

short and well set, and appears to be big with child, can read and write, is a good needle woman and cook, and can wash and iron very well; she says she was born in Charles-town, in South Carolina, and has been in Philadelphia and the island of Grenada. Had on, when she went away, a white Holland jacket, new gray half-thick upper petticoat, and white country kersey under ditto, much worn, with holes in it, osnabrig shift, lawn cap, a white linen handkerchief, or a blue spotted ditto, with holes therein, much worn high heeled leather shoes, with white metal buckles. Whoever takes up the said woman, and secures her, so that her master may get her again, shall receive three pounds reward, if taken more than ten miles from home, and reasonable charges if brought home, paid by George Ashman, junr.

N. B. The aforesaid woman about three years ago was a servant of Mr. Mordecai Gist, in Baltimore town, and is well acquainted there. All masters of vessels are hereby forewarned against carrying her off. [*Maryland Gazette*, May 13, 1773]

[76] Ten Dollars Reward. Run away from the subscriber, living in Morris county, New Jersey, on Sunday night the 9th inst. a likely young Negro wench named Hager, about 20 years old: Had on when she went away, a black and white striped linsey woolsey short gown and petticoat, with some other cloths which she took with her: She has stole some goods, and was under a warrant for stealing when she absented herself. Any person who takes up and secures her, so that she may be had again, shall have the above reward of Ten Dollars, and all reasonable charges, paid by Jacob Morrell. [*New York Gazette*, May 24, 1773]

[77] Twenty Shillings Reward. Ran away last night, from the subscriber, living in Thornbury Township, Chester County, a mulatto wench about 28 or 30 years of age, well set and active; had on and took with her, and India callico gown, and one ditto of brown worsted, a red flannel quilted petticoat, two striped lincey petticoats, two striped lincey short gowns, one worsted and linen ditto, red and yellow mixed, two linen shifts, a pair of thread stockings, and a pair of old high heeled shoes. It is suspected she went off in company with a white man that goes by the name of John May,

but his proper name is Mark Wiley: He is about five feet ten or eleven inches high, slender made, of a pale complexion, has long hair but generally wears a cap over it; had on a white jacket with sleeves, a pair of linen drawers, and other cloaths in a bundle. It is reported he is a deserter from the Royal Irish regiment, and has a wife near Wilmington. Whoever takes up the said wench and secures her, so that her master may have her again, shall have the above reward, and reasonable charges, paid by Persifor Frazer. [*Pennsylvania Packet*, May 24, 1773]

[78] Run away from the subscriber, a convict servant maid, named Sarah Wilson, but has changed her name to Lady Susanna Carolina Matilda, which made the public believe that she was his Majesty's sister, she has a blemish in her right eye, black roll'd hair, stoops in the shoulders, makes a common practice of writing and marking her cloaths with a crown and a B. Whoever secures the said servant woman, or takes her home, shall receive 5 pistoles besides all costs and charges. William Devall. [*Essex Gazette*, May 25, 1773]

[79] Ten Pounds Reward. Run away, last night, three English convict servants, viz. John Eaton, by trade a shipcarpenter, about 23 years of age, and 5 feet 3 or 4 inches high; had on, and took with him, a blue broadcloth coat and breeches, a Damascus waistcoat, a pair of ticken trousers, worsted stockings, three striped cotton shirts, one oznabrig over shirt, a felt hat, and a pair of old shoes. Alice Eaton, alias Walker (who goes for the said John Eaton's wife) a low, well set woman, about 20 years of age, and has sandy coloured hair; had on a brown, stuff gown, a red stuff petticoat, and four red silk handkerchiefs. John Steel, by trade a cabinetmaker, about 18 years of age, 5 feet 5 or 6 inches high, his face is much bruised, and his eyes very black, occasioned by fighting; had on a light coloured waistcoat and breeches, a check shirt, an old hat, and an old pair of shoes, but no stockings. Whoever secures the above servants in any gaol, so that we may get them, shall receive Five Pounds, and if brought to Mr. Sampson Matthews, in Richmond, the above reward. Sampson & George Matthews. [Rind's *Virginia Gazette*, 27 May 27, 1773]

[80] Ran away from the Subscriber, in New-London, on the First Day of Jan. last, an Indian Woman Slave named Mary, about 45 Years old, is very large made, limps with one of her Legs which is sore and much swelled. Had on a black and white drugget Gown. Is supposed to be in or near the Town of Plainfield. All Persons are hereby forbid to entertain, harbour, or have and Kind of Dealings with the said Slave, on Penalty of the Law; and whoever will return her to me shall have Six Shillings Reward. Isaiah Bolles. [*New London Gazette*, May 28, 1773]

[81] Committed to the gaol of Amelia county a Negro woman who says her name is Sukey, but will not, or cannot, tell her master's name; she is a slim wench, and speaks very bad English, her shift is of rolls, and her out dress Virginia cloth. The owner is desired to apply to John Howsin, goaler. [Rind's *Virginia Gazette*, June 3, 1773]

[82] Ran away from the Subscriber last Night, a Negro Woman named Lettice, she's of a very sprightly make, of midling height, and slender built, born upon Long Island, speaks good English, carried with her a coarse purple and white chintz Gown, a strip'd linnen, and a brown worsted Ditto, three strip'd Petticoats, a red tammy Quilt, two new towcloth Shifts, a red broadcloth Cloak, a pair blue cloth Shoes, a black Bonnet, and sundry other articles. Whoever will return said Negro to the Subscriber in Norwich, shall have Two Dollars Reward, and all necessary Charges paid by me Thomas Truman. [*New London Gazette*, June 4, 1773]

[83] Ran away from the subscriber, an English servant girl, named Christiana Ball, but calls herself Caty for shortness; about twenty years of age, brown skinned, black eyes and hair lately cut short, a little stoop shouldered; she has been but a few days in the country. Her cloaths are very ordinary, a brown cloth petticoat, three coarse shifts, and a striped calico short gown; any other cloaths uncertain. Whoever takes her up, and confines her in any gaol within twenty miles of this city, shall have Twenty Shillings reward, or Three Pounds if taken up at any distance further, paid by Henry Neill. [*Pennsylvania Packet*, July 5, 1773]

[84] Run away, on the third of this instant, June, from Thomas Morgan of Newtown, in the County of Bucks, a servant girl named Judith Fagan, a short thick set girl, with black hair, which she commonly wears curled, she is dark complexioned has a bare place on the top of her head about as large as a dollar; had on, and took with her, two short gowns and petticoats, one of a black and blue striped, gown and petticoat of the same; the other short gown and petticoat striped black, blue, red and white, but the red much faded. Who ever takes up said servant and secures her in any goal, so as her master may have her again, shall have three dollars reward and reasonable charges paid by Thomas Morgan. [*Pennsylvania Gazette*, July 16, 1773]

[85] Run away from the Subscriber, on Friday the 9th Day of July Instant, a Molatto Woman Slave nam'd Violetus, aged about 32 Years, of short Stature, and Hair of a yellowish colour: She had with her when she went away a Chints Gown and Cooler, and a Couple of Quilts, one of a blue, the other of a brown Colour, two Pairs of Shoes, and divers other Things. If any Person shall inform where she is, that her Master may have her again, they shall be well rewarded; and all Masters of Vessels and others are hereby warned not to harbour or conceal said Slave.

N. B. It is suspected she is in Company with one Henry Traveller, a free Negro. Abia Keith. [*Boston Evening Post*, July 19, 1773]

[86] Four Dollars Reward. Ran away, June the 20th, from the subscriber living in Middleton Township, Cumberland County, an Irish servant woman, named Eleanor Armstrong, short thick set, brown hair, has a mark on her right cheek received by a cut, about thirty years of age: Had on, and took with her when she went away, a dark calico gown, a white cloth cloak, a black bonnet, three petticoats, a red flannel, a striped linsey and black calimanco, none of them quilted; two shifts, an old and a new; two coarse tow aprons, two pair of black cloth shoes, old blue worsted stockings, a large black silk handkerchief, a red waistcoat, wears a ring on her finger, and smokes tobacco, and it is supposed she has stolen her indenture; she has with her, twenty shillings in money; she landed in

Philadelphia the first of May, says she was married, and her husband died in Philadelphia some short time before she came in; likewise that her husband left money behind him there, and very probable she may have gone there. Whoever takes up the said servant and secures her, so that her master may have her again, shall receive the above reward, and reasonable charges, paid by William Davidson. [*Pennsylvania Packet*, July 26, 1773]

[87] Run away from the subscriber, living in Reading town, Berks county, Pennsylvania, on the 4th day of July, 1773, a certain indented Irish servant woman, named Elizabeth White, about 25 years of age, fair complexion, sandy hair, cut before, about 5 feet high, is very talkative, fond of snuff and spiritous liquors; had on, when she went away, two striped lincey petticoats of one piece, homespun sift, and a silk handkerchief; she may change her apparel, as it is supposed she has money with her; she was seen going towards Philadelphia, and has a brother, in or near the city of New York, named Lee, to which place it is likely she may go. Whoever takes up said servant, and secures her in any goal, so that her master may have her again, shall receive Fifteen Shillings reward, and reasonable charges, paid by Michael Bright. [*Pennsylvania Gazette*, July 28, 1773]

[88] Lancaster Goal, July 28, 1773. This day were committed to my custody, as suspicious persons, a certain John Edwards, alias Jack Mitchel, and Thomas Hutchinson, as they call themselves, and pass for Silversmiths to trade, aged 22 or 23 years each; the said Edwards, alias Mitchel, has a bay Horse, 14 hands high, 7 years old, with a bald face, and a little white on one of his hind feet. Also was committed, a certain Nancy Kean, as she calls herself, and passes for a wife to said Edwards, alias Mitchel; she is a tall thin woman, has black hair, and is pitted with the smallpox; had a dark ground calicoe gown, a black silk apron, a long black silk cardinal, with a lace round it, and a black silk bonnet; she has a young child sucking at her breast, about seven weeks old. Also was committed, a certain Benjamin Smith, alias Harbor, as a strolling vagrant person, has a light blue coat and jacket, with silver buttons, four good shirts, two pair of stockings, and two razors

in a case. At the same time were committed, a certain Peter Grant, and Elizabeth Grant, his wife, as strolling vagrant persons; the said Grant has red hair, is 5 feet 2 inches high, his wife near the same height, very thin, and has a young child sucking at her breast. Also was committed, a certain Margaret McDonnell, as she calls herself, about 30 years of age, 5 feet 6 inches high; had on a red and white linen gown, a green petticoat, and a black bonnet. If any person or persons have any thing to say against any of the above named persons, or any of the described clothes, or the horse, they are desired to send directly to the Justices of the Borough of Lancaster, or come themselves, otherwise the said persons will be discharged, in three weeks from the publication hereof, on paying their fees, by George Eberly, Goaler. [*Pennsylvania Gazette*, August 18, 1773]

[89] Committed to the gaol of Caroline county a Negro woman who calls herself Moll, and says she formerly belonged to Mr. William Bell, at Orange courthouse, and that he sold her to one Mr. Thornton; she is about 4 feet 7 or 8 inches high, and about 35 years old, has two remarkable scars in her face, extending from her eyes downwards, and is cloathed in cotton and brown linen, such as is usually given to Negroes. The owner is desired to pay charges, and take him away. The Gaoler. [Rind's *Virginia Gazette*, August 19, 1773]

[90] Ran away from me the Subscriber, on Tuesday the 13th of May last, a Negro Woman Slave named Nancy: She is a tall Woman, aged about 22 Years, and had on when she went away, a blue and white loose Gown; and did about two Years ago belong to Mr. Samuel Willis of Bridgwater. Whoever shall bring said Runaway to me the Subscriber shall be well rewarded for their Trouble, by Francis Perkins. [*Boston Evening Post*, August 30, 1773]

[91] Five Pounds Reward. Ran away from the subscriber, an Irish servant girl named Mary M'Thownan, but perhaps may change her name; she is about five feet two inches high, a thick set well looking girl, has light brown hair, a short nose, a scar over one of her eyes, and speaks and looks very bold; she had on and took with her, a calico short gown, a striped linen ditto, a red under petticoat,

shade and bonnet of black flowered mode, and a pair of black silk mitts: She stole and took with her, one calico gown of a shell figure, one black calimanco petticoat quilted in flower figure, a white worked border for a petticoat, and a handkerchief of ironed cloaths, containing three white linen shirts marked I. M. one stock marked T. B. and two shifts; one piece of linen of 23 yards, bleacher, Samuel Dunlope, one half johannes, one English guinea, one four or six dollar bill, and sundry small bills not known. Whoever takes up and secures the said servant girl, so that her master may have her again, shall have the above reward, paid by James Brown, Tavern keeper, in Water street, Philadelphia. [*Pennsylvania Packet*, September 6, 1773]

[92] Two Dollars Reward. Run away from the subscriber, living in Upper Salford township, Philadelphia county, on Friday, the 27th of August last, a Dutch servant Girl, named Catherine Thillen, she is about 21 or 22 years of age, of a blackish complexion, with a round full face, black hair, and is a middle sized woman; she came in this country last Christmas, and was sold from on board a vessel to one Charles Pryor, in Philadelphia, and afterwards assigned to the subscriber; she had six years to serve, from the time she came in the country; had on, when she went away, a green woollen woman's jacket, a bluish mixed petticoat, a Dutch calicoe quilted cap, a tow apron, and old shoes; she took two white shirts with her, and sundry other things, not known; she was seen on Skippack road, going to Philadelphia, and says she had friends living there. Whoever takes up said servant, and secures her in the workhouse, in Philadelphia, or in any goal, and gives notice to her master, shall have the above reward, and reasonable charges, paid by Michael Croll. [*Pennsylvania Gazette*, September 8, 1773]

[93] Committed to the gaol of Prince William, the 27th of August, an outlandish Negro woman, speaks English very indifferently, but, as well as I can learn from her, her name is Jenny; she is of the middle size, has on a brown linen shift and petticoat, and is about 25 years old, slim made. The owner is desired to pay charges, and take her away. John Blanset, Gaoler. [Rind's *Virginia Gazette*, September 23, 1773]

[94] Forty Shillings Reward. Run away, on the third of this instant October, from the subscriber, living in Moyamensing township, an Irish servant woman, named Jane McDole, pretty far advanced in her pregnancy, and speaks very broad English, about 17 years of age, 5 feet high, long black hair, fair face, and red cheeks; had on a lincey petticoat, striped with green and black, a yellow under petticoat, with red binding, a homespun shift, with linen sleeves, white apron, white thread stockings, leather shoes, torn across the upper part, a fine cap, with double laced border, a white muslin handkerchief, a redish poplin gown, somewhat stained behind, and a blue silk bonnet. Whoever takes up or secures said servant, so that her master may have her again, shall receive the above reward, and all reasonable charges, paid by George Lesur. [*Pennsylvania Gazette*, October 6, 1773]

[95] Forty Shillings Reward. Run away from the subscriber, living in Burlington, a well-looking Dutch servant woman, named Anna Margarette Freluhen, about 22 years of age, has black hair, swarthy complexion, and pock-marked; carried with her a large bundle of different kinds of Dutch cloaths, likewise her Indentures: She came in the Britannia, Capt. Peters, from Rotterdam, about two weeks since, and cannot talk a word of English. It is thought she will aim for Lancaster or Frederick-town. Whoever takes up the said servant, and secures her in any of his Majesty's gaols, so that her Master may have her again, shall be entitled to the above reward. John Pool. [*Pennsylvania Journal*, October 6, 1773]

[96] Committed to the gaol of Prince William a servant woman about 26 years of age, named Mary Richardson; has on a short printed cotton gown, and striped Virginia cloth petticoat. John Blanchard, Gaoler. [Rind's *Virginia Gazette*, October 14, 1773]

[97] Eight Dollars Reward. Run away, on Sunday, the 26th of September last, from the subscriber, living near Shippensburg, in Cumberland county, the two under-mentioned servants, viz. Michael Jefferies, about 30 years of age, born in Ireland, 5 feet 5 or 6 inches high, well set, has a scar on his right arm, a little below his elbow, likewise a flesh-mark on his right side, near his back; is of a dark complexion, and has dark brown hair; had on, and took

with him, one blue coat without lining, one tow shirt, on pair of tow trowsers, one pair of dark cloth breeches, one pair of stockings, and an old felt hat.

Margaret Jefferies, wife of the above, about 24 years of age, born in Scotland, and speaks broad, has a scar in her forehead, dark complexion, dark brown hair; had on, and took with her, one green quilted petticoat, two striped lincey ditto, one plain lincey jacket, one tow shift, one check apron, one pair of blue stockings, and a pair of leather shoes. Whoever takes up said servants, and secures them in any goal, so that their master may get them again, shall have the above reward, and reasonable charges, paid by John Blyth. [*Pennsylvania Gazette*, October 20, 1773]

[98] Run away from the Subscriber, in Elizabeth City, some Time in June last, a likely Virginia born Negro Wench named Rachel, near thirty years old, about five Feet one or two Inches high, has large Eyes, and the End of one of her fore Fingers broke; she had on a blue Jacket, and an old Cotton Petticoat. I expect she is about Norfolk, or got on Board some Vessel, and gone up James River. Whoever takes up said Negro, and conveys her to me, or confines her in any Jail, so that I get her again, shall have Thirty Shillings Reward. Lockey Collier. [Purdie & Dixon's *Virginia Gazette*, October 21, 1773]

[99] Four Dollars Reward. Run away, in the night of the 27th of October, 1773, from the subscriber, at the upper end of Hunterdon county, West New Jersey, an indented servant girl, named Elizabeth Edgworth, tall and slim built, brown hair; had on, when she went away, a striped short gown, two striped petticoats, a short check apron, no shoes nor stockings. She is supposed to be in or about Philadelphia. Whoever takes up and secures said servant, so that her master may have her again, shall receive the above reward, and reasonable charges, paid by Edward Henderson. [*Pennsylvania Gazette*, November 10, 1773]

[100] Five Dollars Reward. Run away from the subscriber, living in Earl township, Lancaster county, a servant man, Named Robert Chestnut, born in Ireland, and has been in this country seven years; he is about 27 years of age, about 5 feet 6 or 7 inches high,

black hair, brown eyes, fresh complexion; had on, when he went away, a blanket coat, bound with blue ferreting, half-worn, a double breasted jacket, tow trowsers, new shoes, steel buckles, and an old felt hat. He took a young woman with him, who he says is his wife; she is pock-marked, full faced, low size; she had three gowns with her, one orange stuff, one white, and one cotton ditto, and other clothes. Whoever secures the above servant man, so that his master may have him again, shall receive the above reward, paid by John Shovalter, or Mr. Funk, at the Sigh of the Black Bear, in Market street, Philadelphia. [*Pennsylvania Gazette*, November 10, 1773]

[101] Ten Dollars Reward. Run away on Tuesday night, from Michael Varien, a negro wench named Violet, about eighteen years old, of a yellowish colour about five feet high, she has a scar on her left arm where she was inoculated about the size of a shilling and a small blemish in one of her eyes; before she went off she took away a large quantity of chintz gowns, two black silk cloaks and hats, a red short cloak, laced caps, etc. Whoever brings the said wench to the Bull's Head in Bowery Lane shall receive the above reward. [*New York Gazetteer*, November 18, 1773]

[102] Run away from the Subscriber, in Botetourt, three Convicts, viz. David Jones, a Welchman, about forty Years old, and blind of the right Eye; he took away a dark coloured Coat, the Chain Hemp, the Filling Wool doubled, twisted Hemp Shirt and Trousers, and an old Fur Hat. Elizabeth Cowan, a Scotch Woman, about fifty Years old, and of a ruddy Complexion; she had on, and took away with her, a Variety of Petticoats, and Bed Gowns of different Stripes and Colours. William Gray, an Englishman, about 21 Years old, and of a middle Size; he took away a dark coloured Duffil Newmarket Coat, a blue Jacket made Sailor Fashion, Hemp Shirt and Trousers, and new Shoes. It is supposed the old Man and Woman will change their Names, and pass for Man and Wife. Whoever takes said Convicts, and brings them to the Subscribers, shall receive Four Pounds if taken in this County, and Ten Pounds if taken out of it. Caleb Worley. Hugh Allen. [Purdie & Dixon's *Virginia Gazette*, December 2, 1773]

[103] Three Pounds Reward. Run away from the Subscriber, Sept. 8th, 1773, an indented Servant Girl named Mary Kelly, lately from Ireland, but says she has lived 14 Years in London; is about 18 or 20 Years of Age, five Feet six or eight Inches high, stoops in walking, fair Complexion and reddish Hair. Had on when she went away, a little round Man's Hat, green Petticoat, and black Stuff Shoes; took with her two short Gowns, one striped blue and white, the other Callicoe with red Flowers; and six Yards of Callicoe not made. Whoever takes up the said run away Servant, and secures her in any of his Majesty's Goals so that she may be had again, shall be intituled to the above Reward, and if brought home, all reasonable Charges paid by me, G. Barnes. At the Sign of the Harp and Crown, in Wilmington. [*New York Gazette*, December 20, 1773]

1774

[104] Run away the 24th of October, from the subscribers in Philadelphia, two Dutch bound servants, a man and a woman; the man's name is Justus Hornschier, a shoemaker by trade, about 5 feet 7 or 8 inches high, pock marked, has got but one eye; had on when he went away, a blue coat and jacket, and buckskin breeches. The woman's name is Catharine Mum, but it is likely she may alter it to that of the man's, and that they will pass for man and wife; she is about 5 feet high, slender bodied, talks or knows very little English; had on and took with her when she went away, a callicoe short gown, a green camblet gown, two striped camblet petticoats, a Dutch chintz jacket, one white and some ozenbrig aprons, a black bonnet, a white cloth short cloak with a hood to it. Whoever takes up the said servants, and confines them in any gaol, so that their masters may have them again, shall have Three Pounds reward for both, or for the maid alone Forty-five shillings, and all reasonable charges paid by John Roop, and George Leib. [*New York Gazette*, January 17, 1774]

[105] Run away from the subscriber, in October last, a middle sized Negro woman, named Phillis, and was late the property of Counsellor Carter; she is about 35 years of age, has a few specks of black about the lower part of her face, some scars on her breast, and has a very impertinent countenance; she was formerly the property of Mr. Morse, at Poquoson. Her common dress, when she went away, was blue plains. I expect she may be in Norfolk or Hampton.

Whoever secures the above Negro in any of his Majesty's gaols shall receive a reward of twenty shillings from me, in Williamsburg. John Draper. She is fond of liquor, and apt to sing indecent and sailors songs when so. It is probable she will endeavour to pass for a free woman. All masters of vessels and others are hereby forewarned from harbouring the said Negro. [Rind's *Virginia Gazette*, January 27, 1774]

[106] Run away, about the first of November, a Negro Woman, named Rachel, well made, about 22 Years of Age, four Feet eight or nine Inches high, had on when she went away Osnabrug and blue Halfthick Petticoats, a blue and white flowered Linen Waistcoat, and a Felt Hat; she has been brought up in the House, combs her Hair long, endeavouring to impose herself on the Publick for a free Woman, and is apt to change her Name. I purchased her of Mr. Jabez Pitt of Maryland, and expect she will endeavour to get there. Whoever apprehends the said Negro, and conveys her to me, shall have 3 l. Reward, if taken in this Colony, and if in any other 5 l. John Jones. [Purdy & Dixon's *Virginia Gazette*, February 10, 1774]

[107] Run away, the 20th of January last, from the subscriber, living in Oxford township, Chester county, a servant girl, named Margaret Smith, well featured, broad faced, pock-pitted, short rough blackish hair; had on, and took with her, an old black silk cardinal, diced, not trimmed save the cap, an old black silk bonnet, a callicoe gown, striped with a little purple flower, a good deal wore, an old blue quilted petticoat, a lincey petticoat, striped greenish and red, a piece of old lincey, striped blue red and white, which I suppose she will make a bed-gown of, a pair of old calf-skin pumps, lined with linen, coarse blue stockings; she is lusty and talkative, it is like she will pass for a woman with child, and probably is so; she came to this country last summer from Belfast with Captain Ewing; was taken near Lancaster, and sold there to one Mr. Jack, in the Manor of Conestogoe, but returned, and it is likely she has gone that road, as she talked of going to the back woods. Whoever takes up and secures said servant, so that her master may get her again, shall have Four Dollars reward, and reason-

Rachel, a "Negro Woman . . . about 22 Years of age" wears two petticoats, "a blue and white flowered Linen Waistcoat, and a Felt Hat." See advertisement 106 from Purdy & Dixon's *Virginia Gazette*, February 10, 1775. Illustration by Eric H. Schnitzer.

able charges, paid by Thomas Whiteside. [*Pennsylvania Gazette*, February 23, 1774]

[108] Ran away from Ichabod Babcock, of Charlestown, the 16th day of February, 1774, an Indian girl, named Hannah Skesuck, about 15 years of age; she is fat, thick, well set, of a light complexion, thick lips, had on when she went away a flannel shift, an old flannel quilt, a striped flannel petticoat, dark coloured stockings, a striped flannel short gown, and a striped linen cooler: Whoever will take up said girl, and return her to her said master, or secure her so that he may have her again, shall have two dollars reward, and all necessary charges, paid by Ichabod Babcock. [*Newport Mercury*, March 7, 1774]

[109] Run away from the subscriber, in Cumberland county, on the 26th of February, a Mulatto man slave named Sancho, appears to be about 40 years old, stoops a good deal, and is by trade a carpenter and cooper; had on, when he went away, the usual cloathing of Negroes, and carried with him a broadcloth Coat, mixed with something of a violet colour, a blue dual coat and blanket, a large knife, made in the shape of a butcher's, the blade of which is broad, and about 15 inches long. Absconded with him a white servant woman named Elizabeth Beaver, about 20 years old, of a fresh complexion, low, but thick, her hair, being cut in a very uncommon manner, is short, but long about her temples. She went off without either hat or bonnet; but I imagine she now wears a man's hat, as the fellow carried with him two of that sort. She took with her one yarn, one cotton, and one linen striped holland gown, a very good blue calimanco quilt, and many other things. I expect they will change their names, and endeavour to pass for husband and wife, as free people. Whoever will bring the said runaways to me shall receive Six Pounds, if taken in Virginia, and Ten Pounds, if out of it, besides what the law allows. I forewarn all persons from carrying them out of the colony. The fellow is outlawed. Joseph Calland. [Rind's *Virginia Gazette*, March 17, 1774]

[110] Twenty Shillings Reward. Run away from the subscriber, living in Passyunk township, the 12th instant, a Dutch servant woman, named Catherine Moserin, she is about 5 feet high, fresh

coloured, can talk no English, is very fond of rum, and very talkative; had on, when she went away, a white cap, a redish striped silk handkerchief, a red flannel short gown, with black flowers, a dark blue petticoat, the binding of a lighter colour, and new shoes, with white metal buckles. Whoever takes her up, and brings her to her master, shall have the above reward, and reasonable charges, paid by Christian Derick. [*Pennsylvania Gazette*, March 23, 1774]

[111] Two Dollars Reward. Run away the 25th of March, 1774, from the subscriber, living near the Drawbridge, Philadelphia, a Dutch servant girl, named Elizabeth Branet, full faced, and has short black hair; had on, and took with her, a blue Dutch jacket, a striped lincey petticoat, a red serge ditto, a check apron, a coarse white ditto, flat heeled leather shoes, woollen stockings. Whoever takes up said servant, and secures her, so as her master may get her again, shall have the above reward; if above five miles from home, Four Dollars reward, and reasonable charges, paid by John Pinkerton. [*Pennsylvania Gazette*, 30 March 30, 1774]

[112] Committed to the gaol of Prince George two Virginia born negro women; one of which says her name is Milly, about 25 years of age, 5 feet 1 inch high, of a yellow complexion, and has on a striped holland waistcoat, Virginia cloth petticoat, old black quilt, and oznabrig shift; she says she belongs to Mrs. Posey. The other says her name is Betty, about 5 feet 3 inches high, 23 years old, of a yellow complexion, and has on a Virginia cloth gown, white dimity and striped Virginia cloth petticoats, and oznabrig shift; she says she belongs to John Moss. The owners are desired to pay charges, and take them away. The Gaoler. [Rind's *Virginia Gazette*, April 7, 1774]

[113] Run away from Forceput two convict servant women, imported in the Success's Increase last December, which are supposed to have made towards Norfolk, in order to get on board the said ship, as one of them was kept by the second mate, who parted with her with much reluctance, and the other was connected with a silversmith who came passenger, and lives in Norfolk, and who would have married her if her temper had not been too disagreeable; her name is Susanna Ball, is a small woman, of a thin

visage, has black hair, and has on a new pompadour gown, quilted coat, stays, leather pumps, and a black sattin hat; she took with her an old green gown, brown quilted coat, check, white blue, and brown linen aprons, coloured handkerchiefs, linen and muslin caps, worsted and thread stockings. The other is called Anne Ellis, a full faced, lusty woman, of a ruddy complexion, has black hair, and is much addicted to swearing; had on, and took with her, a black stuff gown, callico gown, and bed gown, a black petticoat, check and brown linen aprons, Virginia shoes, with leather heels, and worsted stockings. She has both gold and silver with her. Whoever will deliver the above women at Forceput, about six miles from Fredericksburg, shall receive Five Pounds, or one of the women, if the money is not paid in twenty four hours after demand. H. Grymes. [Rind's *Virginia Gazette*, April 7, 1774]

[114] Run away from the Subscriber, in Charlotte County, on Little Roanoke, a Negro Man named Tom, of a yellowish Complexion, about thirty Years old, middle sized, has a long thin Visage, a low effeminate Voice, two of his fore Teeth a little decayed, and one Eye is smaller than the other, occasioned probably by some old Hurt; had on, when he went away, old Virginia Cloth Jacket and Breeches, which are probably wore out by this Time. Run away also, a likely Negro Woman named Fanny, of a black Complexion, about 25 Years old, has a small Scar on one of her Cheeks, and the Mark of a Switch on one of her Arms; she had a blue Jacket, and a Petticoat very much patched. They are Man and Wife, and will probably go down to Gloucester County, from whence they originally came. A Reward of Five Pounds will be given for conveying them to Drury Yeoman. [Purdie & Dixon's *Virginia Gazette*, April 14, 1774]

[115] Twenty Shillings Reward. Run away, on the 30th of last March, from the subscriber in Fourth street, near the Post office, an apprentice girl, named Anne Carrowle, came from London with Captain William Keais, in the year 1769, she has a fresh complexion, brown hair, near sighted, left handed, round shouldered, and about 16 years of age; had on, when she went away, a green silk bonnet, an India red and black and white calicoe long gown, a blue

halfthicks, and striped lincey petticoat, a white apron, and new leather shoes; she has been seen strolling on the Lancaster and Gulf roads, on pretence of going to service at Esquire Moore, and the Bull Tavern, and then at Carlisle. Whoever takes up the above runaway, and secures her, so as her master may get her again, shall have the above reward; and all persons are cautioned not to conceal or entertain her. Samuel Williams. [*Pennsylvania Gazette*, April 27, 1774]

[116] Run away from the Subscriber, in March last, a likely Virginia born Wench named Betty, about 22 Years of Age, stout and well set, wears Silver Earrings set with white Stone, and carried with her several Suits of Clothes. She was formerly the Property of Mr. James Mitchell, deceased, at York, and has been used to attend in a Publick House from her Infancy. She has been seen at several Places on James River, but last at Captain William Acrill's, in Charles City, where I am informed she has several Relations. Any Person that will secure the said Slave, so that I get her again, shall have Three Pounds Reward. Hardin Burnley. [Purdie & Dixon's *Virginia Gazette*, May 12, 1774]

[117] Ran away from the Subscriber, on the 23d Instant, a Melatto Wench named Kate, about 23 Years old, born in the Country; she's tall and likely to look to, has bushy Hair, and dresses neat: Had on when she went off, a dark striped homespun Gown, black calamanco Quilt, check'd Apron, red broadcloth Cloak, black Satten Hat, and round silver Shoe-Buckles. Whoever will take up said Wench, and return her to the Subscriber in New-London, or secure her so that she may be had, shall have Ten Dollars Reward, and all necessary Charges paid by me Robinson Mumford. [*New London Gazette*, May 13, 1774]

[118] Ten Pounds Reward. Run away from the subscriber, in Botetourt, on the night of the first instant (May) two convict servants, viz. John Jones, a shoemaker, born in Liverpool, but I believe can speak Welsh, of a yellow Complexion, brown hair, a large nose, and pitted with the small pox, about 36 years of age, 5 feet 8 inches high, round shouldered, thick made, stoops much in his walk, and has a scar on his right leg, occasioned by a wound

when he followed the sea; had on, and took with him, a light coloured sailor's jacket, fearnought breeches, two shirts of country made linen, a pair of trousers, and osnabrigs to make another pair. I also miss a new pair of buckskin breeches, with John Stewart wrote on the inside of the waistband, which I suspect he has taken. Elizabeth Lewellin, a Welsh woman, about 25 years of age, 5 feet 6 inches high, black hair, full faced, fresh and lusty, wants one of her fore teeth, and has a very remarkable scar on her throat; had on, and took with her, a new calico gown that buttons before, black calimanco petticoat and shoes, an old pair of green coloured stays, new striped country made linsey bedgown and petticoat, and sundry other clothes. She is smart and active, and capable of any business, can read and write, and probably may forge a pass. She has, I am informed, a sum of money which she brought into the country; and I imagine they will make for a seaport, as the man formerly followed the sea. Whoever takes up and secures the said servants, so that I get them again, shall have the above reward, besides what the law allows; and I forewarn all masters of vessels, and others, from carrying them off at their peril. Patrick Lockhart. [Purdie & Dixon's *Virginia Gazette*, May 26, 1774]

[119] Run away the 21st Instant, from the Subscriber, in Albemarle, on North River, near the Brokenback Church, a large well set Mulatto woman Slave named Bess, but calls herself Betty Sanders, about 21 Years of Age, with a small Scar on one of her Arms; had on, and carried with her, a striped Country Cloth Waistcoat and Petticoat, white Cotton Shift and Bonnet a red Handkerchief, a Pair of Mens turned Pumps, and a Pair of Thread Stockings, one of them Country knit. Whoever takes up the said Slave and delivers her to me, or secures her in any Jail so that I get her again, shall have 40 s. Reward, besides what the Law Allows. John Alloway Strange.

N. B. It is supposed she went off with a white Man. [Purdy & Dixon's *Virginia Gazette*, June 2, 1774]

[120] Eight Dollars Reward. Ran away last night, from the subscriber, two Dutch servants; the one a lusty woman, named Joanna Vanderstien, much pitted with the small pox, has a sour down

look, the middle finger of her right hand has the end mashed off; had on when she went away, an India calico gown, blue and white striped lincey petticoat, black Persian bonnet, and good shoes; she took with her two striped short gowns, two white aprons, and other cloaths that cannot be described: She has a constant bad cough attending her. The other a lad, named John Valentine Kimberger, between 18 and 19 years of age, a clever smart looking boy, has light brown curled hair, is a little pitted with the small pox, and when spoke to pretty quick seems to be frightened; had on a light coloured fustian frock coat, a brown cotton velvet jacket, coarse white shirt, coarse trowsers, and good new shoes; took with him a pair of light coloured knit breeches, a good white shirt, several coarse old ones, and a white dimity jacket: Neither of the above servants speak good English. Whoever takes up and secures the said servants, so that their master may have them again, shall have the above Reward, and reasonable charges, paid by Davis Bevan. [*Pennsylvania Packet*, June 13, 1774]

[121] Run away from the Subscriber, in York County, the 17th Instant (June) a small Mulatto Wench about fifteen Years old, named Sall, who took with her all her Wearing and Bed Clothes, amongst which were several Dutch Blankets. There went off with her, as her Husband, a Mulatto Fellow belonging to John Hatley Norton, Esq; and as they were seen to go by Colonel Harwood's Mill, I have Reason to believe they are lurking about Williamsburg or Jamestown. Whoever secures the said Wench, so that I get her again, shall have 20 s. Philip Dedman. [Purdie & Dixon's *Virginia Gazette*, June 16, 1774]

[122] Run away from the Subscriber, in Buckingham a Negro Woman named Bess; had on, and carried with her, a green Calimanco Petticoat, a striped Holland Waistcoat, a Negro Cotton Petticoat, a Virginia Cloth one striped with Copperas and filled in with blue Yarn, two Osnabrug Shifts one new, the other old. Whoever brings the said Negro to me, at Buckingham Courthouse, shall have 5 l. Reward if taken in Carolina, and 40 s. if in Virginia, besides what the Law allows. Archelaus Austin. [Purdy & Dixon's *Virginia Gazette*, July 21, 1774]

[123] Ran away from her Master, Francis Shaw, a likely tall Negro Woman, known by the Name of Violet Shaw, about 25 Years old; has a Blemish in one Eye, carried away with her a white Calico Riding Dress, a strip'd Calico Gown, a Claret colour'd Poplin Gown, a strip'd blue and white Holland Gown, a Bengal Gown, and many other valuable Articles of Apparel. Whoever apprehends her, and will return her to her Master in Boston, shall have Four Dollars Reward and all necessary Charges paid. All Persons are cautioned against harbouring, or carrying off said Negro Servant as they would avoid the Rigor of the Law. [*Boston Evening Post*, August 1, 1774]

[124] Run away on the 3d of this instant (August) from my quarter, on Carter's Run, a negro wench named Winney; she is about eighteen or twenty years of age, 5 feet 3 or 4 inches high, of a yellowish complexion, had on when she went away an oznabrig shift, petticoat, and jacket; she also took with her a white dowlas jacket and petticoat, and a great variety of other clothes. She being an artful, subtle wench, I imagine will frequently change her dress. I do not recollect any particular mark she has in her face, though I am told there is a lump upon the back of her neck, occasioned by the cut of a switch. About three years ago she made an elopement, and got into Maryland, near Port Tobacco, where she passed several months for a free woman, and went by the name of Winney Redman. Whoever will take up the said wench, and deliver her to me, in Facer county, near the courthouse, or to my overseer on Carter's Run, in the said county, shall receive Twenty Shillings reward, if taken up in the said county, if in the adjacent counties Forty Shillings, if out of the colony Five Pounds, besides what the law allows, and all reasonable charges paid. James Scott, junior. [Rind's *Virginia Gazette*, August 25, 1774]

[125] Run away from her Master, Joseph Goldthwait of Weston, a Maid Servant named Sarah Naffell, about thirty Years of Age, born in Guernsey; had on when she went away, a dark short Gown, a brown Petticoat, and carried with her a long dark Gown of crossbarr'd Stuff, with some Linen; is of a middling Stature and speaks a little broken. Whoever will take her up and convey her to her

Master at Weston, shall have Four Dollars Reward, and all reasonable Charges paid by Jos. Goldthwait. [*Boston Evening Post*, September 5, 1774]

[126] Eight Dollars Reward. Run away, the 20th of June, from the subscriber, an Irish servant girl, named Ann Carson, about 25 years old, middle size, chunky made, swarthy complexion, the backs of her hands much swelled, supposed to be with child, pale smooth face, brown hair; had on a sprigged short calicoe gown, black calimancoe skirt, an under petticoat, with a calicoe border. It is supposed she is gone to a certain John Heron, who lives in Donegall township, Lancaster county, as she was seen going that road, and said Heron came in the ship Prosperity, Captain McCullock, from Belfast, with said servant, last May. Whoever secures said servant, and lodges her in goal, so that her master may get her again, shall be entitled to the above reward, and reasonable charges, if brought home to Edward Hanlon, in Walnut street, Philadelphia. [*Pennsylvania Gazette*, September 7, 1774]

[127] Eight Dollars Reward. Yesterday absented from her master, a Scotch indented servant girl, named Martha M'Loud, about 18 years of age, a likely well set person, of a fair complexion; light coloured hair, cut short; had on, when she went away, a round-ear'd cap, cross-barred charlotte gown, of brown and white colours, intermixed with green and white flowers, a blue worsted skirt, two red petticoats, one of which is fine serge, a pair of old buckskin shoes, and white worsted stockings; she lately lived with a certain Alexander Chisholm, Innkeeper, in Burlington, who assigned her to George Bartam, merchant, in Philadelphia, and was by him assigned to me, the first day of this instant. Whoever apprehends said servant, and delivers her to her master, the subscriber, or secures her so as she may be had again, shall receive three pounds reward, and reasonable charges paid by John Zell. [*New York Journal*, October 6, 1774]

[128] Forty Shillings Reward. Run away from the subscribers, two Scotch indented servants, viz. a woman about 22 years of age, named Isabel M'Arthur, of a ruddy complexion, pitted with the small pox, dark brown hair, and dark eyes; speaks very bad

English: Had on when she went away, a strip'd cotton short gown, a homespun petticoat, and a black bonnet; it is very probable she may change her dress, as she took with her, a green gown, and one of Scotch plaid, with several short gowns of Scotch stuff. The other a man, named Alexander Morrison, about 40 years of age, red hair, remarkably clumsy ancles, and crooked feet. Whoever will secure the said servants, so that their masters may have them again, shall receive the above reward, or Twenty Shillings for either, paid by Abraham Messier, Ralph Thurman. [*New York Journal*, October 13, 1774]

[129] Ran away from the subscriber, on the 26th inst. an apprentice girl, named Jane Fontena, about 19 years of age; had on when she went away, a red damask gown, green stuff quilted coat, a long brown cloak, and a black bonnet: All persons are cautioned against secreting, or harbouring, said runaway, as they would avoid being prosecuted for the same; and any person securing said Jane Fontena, and conveying her to the subscriber, shall have one dollar reward, and all necessary charges paid by William Selby. [*Newport Mercury*, October 31, 1774]

[130] Five Dollars Reward. Run away from the subscriber, living in Little Dock street, near the Counties-Market, yesterday morning, a Scotch servant girl, named Jane M'Creddie, she is 25 yeas of age, about 5 foot 3 inches high, pretty much pitted with the small-pox, well set, speaks very much the Scotch Dialect, and came from Greenock in September last: She had on and took with her when she went away, a short camblet gown with green, red and yellow stripes, a green callimancoe quilted petticoat, a long gown about the same colour of the short one, a new black satten bonnet lined with blue ribbons on the crown; what is most remarkable, she has a scar on one hand and thumb. John Myford. [*New York Gazette*, December 26, 1774]

1775

[131] Twenty Shillings Reward. Run away, on the 24th of December last, from the subscriber, living in Merion, Philadelphia county, a servant girl, named Elizabeth Creely; had on, and took with her, when she went away, a light coloured gown, two gowns like calicoe, a black petticoat, two pair of shoes, one low heeled the other stuff, two pair of stockings, one pair cotton the other silk, and a large blue cloth cloak; she has a round face, and is of a middle size. Whoever takes up the said servant, and secures her, so that her master may have her again, shall have the above reward, paid by John Jones, Merchant, near the Swedes Church, or Hugh Jones. [*Pennsylvania Gazette*, January 4, 1775]

[132] Stop Thief! Stop Thief! Twelve Dollars Reward. Whereas a certain pretended Lady, now known and called by the name of Mary Wenwood, formerly called Mary Butler, a Native of Marblehead, a very lusty Woman much pitted with the Small-Pox, who generally wears the best of Cloathing, did some Time past, take, steal and carry away from my Dwelling-House in Newport, a Woman's red Broad Cloth Cloak and Head, a Muff and Tippet, a Silk Skirt, and sundry other Articles. I do hereby offer a Reward of the said Sum of Twelve Dollars to any Person or Persons who will apprehend the said Mary and confine her in his Majesty's Goal in Newport, exclusive of all reasonable Charges, that he or they may be reasonably at in performing the same. Godfrey Wenwood. [*Boston Post Boy*, January 9, 1775]

[133] Thirty Shillings Reward. Ran away last night, from the subscriber at Brandywine Bridge, near Wilmington, Newcastle county, an Irish servant girl named Margaret Stafford, of a low stature
and well set, brown complexion and round face, about seventeen
years of age; had on and took with her a striped calico gown and
petticoat, a striped lincey petticoat and old quilt, two striped bed
gowns, one lincey and the other linen, two Russia linen shifts, an
old cloth cloak of a drab colour, blue yarn stockings, old black stuff
shoes, and no head dress except caps, that is known of, but may
probably get some, as it is suspected she has some confederate.
Whoever takes up said servant and secures her so that her master
may get her again, shall have the above Reward, and reasonable
charges, paid by William Starr. [*Pennsylvania Packet*, January 9,
1775]

[134] Whereas my wife Sarah Procter has eloped from me, with a
certain John Orr, I therefore do hereby forewarn all persons not to
trust her on my account, for I will pay no debts of her contracting
from the date hereof.

N. B. The said John Orr is about 19 years of age, 5 feet 8 or 9
inches high, slim made, with a down look, and brown hair tied
behind; he is scaley skinned, as through he had the scurvy; had on,
when he went away, a blue cloth coat, a white linen jacket, light
coloured plush breeches, much worn, a new fur hat, a red flag
handkerchief round his neck. Said Orr has a note for Five Pounds,
on Isaac Berns and me; I hereby forewarn all persons from taking
any assignment on said note, as we think that we have no right to
pay it. The abovesaid Sarah Procter is a middle sized woman, has
brown hair; had on a worsted gown, of a lead colour, a small spotted calicoe bed gown, a blue calimancoe quilt, a black bonnet,
light coloured cloth shoes, and is about five months gone with
child; she is a sieve weaver by trade. Whoever will give me satis-
factory intelligence, so as I can get to see them, shall have the
reward of Four Dollars, John Procter. [*Pennsylvania Gazette*,
January 11, 1775]

[135] Run away from the subscriber, living at Brooke's Bank, in
Essex county, on the 14th of this instant, a likely mulatto girl
named Peg, about 15 or 16 years of age, and of a middle size; had

on when she went away a brown linen jacket and petticoat, plaid stockings, common shoes, a calico jacket and petticoat, 1 or 2 white linen shifts, and several other clothes, which I do not remember. She was brought up as a house servant, and understands that business well. When she is taxed for committing any fault, she appears to be greatly surprized, and is apt to cry. The same evening she went away she was seen to go on board a sloop at Layton's warehouses; when she hailed the sloop, she told the skipper, who was a white man, that her name was Dinah, and that she wanted to go to Norfolk or to be set ashore on the other side of the river. The skipper sent his flat and two negroes and carried her on board, about sun-set. This information I had from the sailors on board captain Martin's ship, who saw all that passed. I am inclined to believe she was prevailed on to go off, as she went away without the least provocation, and never was guilty of the like before. She was born where I live, and never was 5 miles from home. If carried off by any vessel, I will give 5 l. reward to the person who brings her back, and 10 l. more to know the skipper of such vessel, so that I may have him taken; and if taken strolling about any where, I will give the same, and pay reasonable charges. Richard Hipkins. [Pinckney's *Virginia Gazette*, January 12, 1775]

[136] Three Pounds Reward. Ran away from the Subscriber, on the 1st of January, a middling dark Mulatto named Stephen, about 21 Years of Age, and thick made; had on, when he went off, a Negro Cotton Waistcoat and Breeches, an Osnabrug Shirt, and Negro made Shoes, with Pegs drove in the Soals; his Hair is cut off the Top of his Head, and but little remains at the Sides. He carried with him a white Mulatto Woman Slave named Phebe, whose Hair is long, straight, and black; she had on a blue Waistcoat and Petticoat, and took with her two new Osnabrug Shirts, and a Suit of striped Virginia Cloth; she is about 21 Years of Age. They also carried off two Osnabrug Shirts, 6 or 7 Ells of Rolls, a new Dutch Blanket, and one about Half worn. It is imagined they will make for Carolina; and endeavour to pass for free People. All Persons are forewarned from harbouring them, at their Peril. Whoever brings them to me, or secures them in any Gaol, so that I may get them again, shall have the above Reward. Henry Hardaway. [Dixon & Hunter's *Virginia Gazette*, January 21, 1775]

[137] Six Pence Reward. Run away from the subscriber, a servant girl, named Catherine Keeler, about 17 years of age, well grown; had on, and took with her, a short green baize gown, a brown worsted quilt, two lincey petticoats, two pair of stockings, one check apron, one flag handkerchief, 3 ditto spotted and check linen; she has been lame in one of her big toes, and wore a red flannel on it. Whoever takes up said servant, and secures her in any of his Majesty's goals, shall be intitled to the above reward, and their labour for their pains. Robert Tomkins. [*Pennsylvania Gazette*, January 25, 1775]

[138] Run away last night, from the subscriber, an Irish servant girl, named Mary Simonton, about 26 years of age, about 5 feet 3 or 4 inches high, pitted with the smallpox, full mouthed, very talkative, and talks middling broad; had on and took with her two striped lincey petticoats, one of them new, the other pretty much worn, one blue worsted ditto, one calicoe bed gown, one lincey and one linen ditto, two old and two new shifts, leather heeled shoes, newly soaled, and a testament that she brought from Ireland with her. Whoever takes up said servant, and secures her, so that her master may get her again, shall have Twenty Shillings reward, and reasonable charges, paid by Isaac Tremble. [*Pennsylvania Gazette*, 30 January 30, 1775]

[139] Two Dollars Reward. Ran Away from the subscriber, on the 11th inst. (February) a servant girl named Elizabeth Smith, lately arrived from Liverpool, about eighteen years of age, a little pitted with the small pox, lightish hair, had one when she went away, a green bays short gown and petticoat, an old red cloak and straw hat. Whoever secures said girl and brings her home, shall have the above reward, and reasonable charges. Richard Footman. [*Pennsylvania Packet*, February 27, 1775]

[140] Forty Shillings Reward. Ran away on the 25th of February last, from the subscriber, living in Kent county, Maryland, an English servant woman named Ann Burdon, about 22 years old, lusty and full faced, with brown hair; had on and took with her when she went away, a striped lincey petticoat and jacket, a pair of mens shoes and a pair of yarn stockings; she likewise had three

aprons, two of rapping and the other check. Any person that will take up the said servant woman and secure her in any of his Majesty's gaols, shall have Twenty Shillings if taken in the county, if out of the county Thirty Shillings, and if out of the province the above reward, paid by Benjamin Collins. [*Pennsylvania Packet*, March 6, 1775]

[141] Run away from the Subscriber, about the first of January last, a very bright Mulatto Man named Stephen, 5 Feet 6 or 7 Inches high, about 22 Years of Age, well set, has a remarkable broad Face, with a Mole on the Side of his Nose, and a Scar upon one of his Legs. He was clothed in Negro Cotton Waistcoat and Breeches, Osnabrug Shirt, and a Pair of Blue Gambadoes; his Hair is cut close off the Top of his Head, and the Front Part combed back. His Wife Phebe went away with him, a remarkable white Indian Woman, about the same Age, and was with Child; she has long black Hair, which is generally clubbed, and carried off with her a blue Negro Cotton Waistcoat and Petticoat, a Virginia Cloth Waistcoat and Petticoat, and a Virginia Cloth Bonnet. She can spin well, and I imagine they will both endeavour to pass as free. Whoever apprehends the said Slaves, and brings them to me, in Dinwiddie, near the Courthouse, or secures them in Gaol, so that I get them again, shall have 10 l. Reward from Henry Hardaway. [Dixon & Hunter's *Virginia Gazette*, March 11, 1775]

[142] Run away last October, a middle sized Negro Wench named Hannah, she pokes her Neck out very much, is long thin visaged, and wants an upper fore Tooth, had on a Check Petticoat, one brown Linen Ditto, and a blue Stuff Jump Jacket. She may probably be lurking about Occoquan Works, or at Mr. William Bailey's Quarter in Loudoun, as she had a Husband at each. Whoever brings her home shall receive 3 l. Reward if taken in the Colony, if in any other Colony, 10 l. Gowry Waugh. [Dixon & Hunter's *Virginia Gazette*, March 25, 1775]

[143] Run Away from the Subscriber, a Negro Wench, named Tena, lately the Property of Mr. James King: She had on when she went away, a blue Negro Cloth Gown, and Osnabrugs Apron. She took with her, a great Variety of Cloaths, such as Chintzes,

Callicoes, &c. which, for the Sake of Change, she may appear in; having a Number of Acquaintances and Relations about Town, where, in all Probability, she may be harboured. If she will return, within a Week or ten Days, to her Duty, she shall be forgiven; otherwise a Reward of Ten Pounds will be given, on Delivery of her, to me, or the Warden of the Work-House: And, a further Reward of Fifty Pounds, to any Person or Persons, that can give any Information of her being harboured by a white Person; and Twenty Pounds, if by a Negro. William Roberts. [*South Carolina Gazette*, March 17, 1775]

[144] Forty Shillings Reward. Run away the 25th of March, at 8 o'clock in the evening, an Irish servant maid, named Sarah Clarke (alias Stanley) between 25 and 30 years of age; had on when she went away, a green baize short gown and a black petticoat, also a red under petticoat, with a pair of black stockings, and a pair of old shoes; she also took with her a pair of shoes, lined with red flannel, belonging to her mistress, also a small red striped long gown, with black spots between the stripes, mended under the arms with another sort of calico, likewise an old dark nap cloak; she has no bonnet on, as she has commonly a ribbon round her head; she is of a middle stature, fat and clumsy, her face has some little purple spots; she is fresh coloured, a cut in her forehead, also darkish hair and very thin, and looks very suspicious of being with child; she has been married to a soldier in Ireland. Whoever takes up and secures said servant, so that her master may get her again, shall have the above reward, and reasonable charges, paid by Joseph Cauffman, in Second street, near Race street.

N. B. She came last fall from Ireland, with Captain Brice, and is supposed to be gone towards Maryland or New York: All masters of vessels, or others, are forbid to harbour or carry her off at their peril. [*Pennsylvania Gazette*, March 29, 1775]

[145] Run away on the 13th instant, from the subscriber living in New London township, Chester county, a native Irish servant girl, named Cicely Morgan, of a small stature, and much given to smoaking, of a sandy complexion, pretty much freckled, and pitted with the smallpox; had on and took with her, a chip hat cov-

ered with black silk, a calico gown with broad stripes and stamped between the stripes with red and black, three petticoats, one lincey, with small brown and white stripes, one ditto green stuff, one ditto reddish, a tow cloth shift, a pair of blue stockings, footed with light blue, a pair of leather heeled shoes tied with strings; also a short gown of a dark colour, and a check apron. Whoever takes up said servant, so that her master may have her again, shall have a reward of Four Dollars, and reasonable charges, paid by me Samuel Floyd. [*Pennsylvania Gazette*, March 29, 1775]

[146] Three Pounds Reward. Run away from the subscriber, living in Swanson street, near the Sign of St. Patrick, an indented servant woman, named Jane Jackson, about 23 or 24 years of age, about 5 feet 2 inches high, a stout fat woman, came from Ireland about the 27th of July last in Captain McClenahans ship; she is an artful sly body, perhaps may pass for a married woman, as some fellow has carried her off; had on, when she went away, an old light blue quilt, patched with brown calimancoe, and lined with narrow striped lincey, a brown bearskin short gown; took with her two blue and white striped homespun short gowns, one not quite made, a black and white long calicoe gown, 2 or 3 check handkerchiefs, a narrow striped new check apron, a new black pelong bonnet, with black lace round it, almost wore out, and many other things unknown. Whoever secures the said servant, so that her master may have her again, shall receive the above reward, and all reasonable charges, paid by Jacob Jones. [*Pennsylvania Gazette*, April 5, 1775]

[147] Philadelphia, May 8, 1775. Twenty Shillings Reward. Ran away last night, from the subscriber, an indented servant Irish woman, known by the name of Leany Brown, perhaps she may call herself Leonora Hamilton, she came to this place last Summer with Capt. M'Cullough, is lusty, fat, and strong made, about five feet seven inches high, round face, a little pitted with the small pox, brown complexion, with a high colour in her cheeks, blue eyes, a good set of teeth, dark brown hair, very talkative, with a little of the brogue on her tongue, and about 30 years of age: She had on a black pasteboard bonnet, trimmed with ribbon and lace, a brown

calimanco gown, blue worsted quilt, a pair of leather or purple velvet shoes, with square carved yellow shoe buckles and thread stockings. Whoever takes up and secures said servant woman that I may get her again, shall receive the above reward, from Daniel Williams. [*Pennsylvania Packet*, May 22, 1775]

[148] Run away from the subscriber, living in Beekman street, in the city of New York, the 27th May, a servant girl named Anne Cooper, born in Scotland, and came from there thirteen months ago, and is about 23 years of age, middling stature, broad shoulders, fresh complexion, (apt to turn pale when angry) long visage, marked with the small pox, small black eyes: had on and took with her when she went away, a black silk hat lined with white silk, a short holland gown, one long gown black and red sprig India callicoe, three plain muslin caps, four handkerchiefs, one a red and white speckled cotton, a gauze, a linen, and one a lawn, a lawn apron, two homespun coarse shifts, one pair of coarse linen hose, a pair of shoes, black flesh, half worn, with one pair pinchbeck buckles, &c. Any person that secures said servant girl, so as her master can have her again, shall have Twenty Shillings reward if taken within this city, elsewhere forty shillings, and all reasonable charges to be paid by Thomas Steele. [*New York Gazette*, June 5, 1775]

[149] Run away, May 20, 1775, from the subscriber, living in York town, an Irish servant girl, named Elizabeth Young, of a dark complexion, low in stature, and has brown hair; she appears as if she was with child; she is a great smoaker of tobacco; had on, and took with her, one small striped blue and white linen short gown and petticoat, one pale blue worsted gown without sleeves, one fine shift half-worn, with robins and Dresden lace round the neck, 3 check aprons, two of them too long for her, one old black quilted petticoat, one pair blue yarn stockings, with some blue cotton in the feet, leather shoes lined with linen, yellow carved metal buckles, one single Kenting handkerchief flowered, one old calicoe short gown, and one white ditto, with pieces set under their arms. It is supposed she has gone with some fellow, and will pass for his wife. Whoever takes up said girl, and secures her, so that her mas-

Elizabeth Young, an "Irish servant girl," was "a great smoaker of tobaccco." She wears a "small striped blue and white linen short gown and petticoat," a "check apron . . . too long for her" over an "old black quilted petticoat." Around her neck is a "Kenting handkerchief flowered." See advertisement 149 from the *Pennsylvania Gazette*, June 14, 1777. Illustration by Eric H. Schnitzer.

ter may have her again, shall have Three Pounds reward, and reasonable expences, paid by William White. [*Pennsylvania Gazette*,
June 14, 1775]

[150] Ran away from the Subscriber, living in Almon-street,
Southwark, Philadelphia, the fourteenth instant, A Servant Girl,
named Mary Brine, about seventeen Years of Age, short and thick
set, pleasant when talking, a little pitted with the Smallpox, had
on a Purple and white short Gown, green Skirt, black Bonnet,
white Handkerchief, and barefooted. Whoever takes up said
Servant, and secures her in any of his Majesty's Jails, shall have
Two Dollars Reward if in the City; if out of it Four Dollars, and all
reasonable Charges. John Douglas. [*Pennsylvania Evening Post*, June
15, 1775]

[151] Ran away from the subscriber, living in Frederick county, on
the 15th of April last, an Irish servant named Peter Kelly, but has
changed his name to Peirce Burn, and has a pass for that purpose;
he is about 5 feet 8 inches high, has dark brown hair, and of a dark
complexion, and down look, this apparel is a light coloured country cloth coat, 1 Holland shirt, 2 osnabrigs ditto, blue yarn stockings with shoes and buckles, a felt hat bound with black worsted
binding, striped linen trousers; also went with him a lusty negro
woman named Rhoad, now goes by the name of Nancy Bannaker,
her apparel a white humhums gown, her other clothing such as is
common for slaves. Whoever takes up said servant and slave, and
secures them, so that their master gets them again, shall if taken
in this province, be intitled to 20 dollars reward, and if out, the
sum of ten pounds, including what the law allows, paid by
Abidnigo Hyatt. [*Maryland Gazette*, June 15, 1775]

[152] Run away from Edenton, in North Carolina, on the 27th of
April last, a negro wench, named Road, about 28 years of age. She
was born in New England, and speaks in that dialect, has remarkable thick lips, wears her hair combed over a large roll, and affects
gaiety in dress. She had on, and took with her, a homespun striped
jacket, a red quilted petticoat, a black silk hat, a pair of leather
shoes, with wooden heals, a chintz gown, and a black cloak. She is

supposed to have a forged pass, and may endeavour to pass as a free woman, and change her clothes and name. Whoever will take up the said wench, and return her to the subscriber, or to Joseph Blunt, esquire, of Edenton, or to Keder Merchant, esquire, of Currituck, or secure her in any of his majesty's gaols, and notify the owner, shall Receive Forty Shillings reward, and reasonable charges, by Josiah Hall. [Pinkney's *Virginia Gazette*, June 15, 1775]

[153] Run away from the Subscriber, in King and Queen, the 5th of October 1774, a Negro Woman named Hannah, of the Middle Stature, remarkably black, has been hurt in one Side (I think the right) which makes her limp as she walks; had on, when she went away, a Negro Cotton Jacket, and a Virginia Cloth Petticoat, striped with black Yarn. Whoever secures her so that I may get her again (if in this Colony) shall have 40 s. Reward, and if out there-of 5l. John Cardwell. [Dixon & Hunter's *Virginia Gazette*, June 17, 1775]

[154] Run away, last night, from the subscriber, an Irish servant woman, named Jane Shepherd, about 24 years of age, has been very stout, but fell away vastly by being under the Doctors care, has black hair, one of her eyes always watering, and has often a sore leg; had on, when she went off, a gown with large red flowers, a lincey petticoat, with small stripes, and a black durant quilted ditto, a white linen apron, about half-worn, and a pair of new black waxed calfskin shoes; she has very black teeth occasioned by smoaking: It is supposed she will change her name and dress, as she had run away before and was apprehended. Whoever takes up said woman, and secures her in any goal, so that her master may have her again, shall have Thirty Shillings reward, and reasonable charges, paid by Michael Swoope.

N. B. She is supposed to be in Cranbury, with a young Irishman, named Thomas Johnston, about 5 feet 6 inches high, has red hair; and a young woman, named Elizabeth Young, about 22 years of age, of a middle size, a servant to William White, of Yorktown, who has advertised Three Pounds reward for taking her up. [*Pennsylvania Gazette*, June 23, 1775.]

[155] Committed to the Gaol of Henrico, a Negro Woman, who says her Name Is Betty, about 4 Feet 10 Inches high; has on an Osnabrug Shift and Petticoat, has a hole through each ear, appears to be outlandish, and cannot tell her Master's Name. The Owner is desired to prove his Property, pay Charges, and take her away. Mary Lindsey, Gaoler. {Dixon & Hunter's *Virginia Gazette*, June 24, 1775]

[156] Forty Shillings Reward. Run away from the Subscriber last Friday, an indented servant woman named Ann Hill, said she was born in Philadelphia, has been in Ireland and England, and is about thirty years of age; took with her, a purple sprigged new callico gown, a red sprigged old ditto, a green moreen ditto, 1 black satin cloak edged with ermine, 1 black mode hat, with blue lining and narrow lace; 1 black bonnet, 1 green moreen, 1 small purple sprigged callico, 1 homespun, and 1 much worn quilted petticoats; 1 fine, and a coarse new shifts; 1 flowered bordered kenting, 1 white linen, and 1 muslin aprons. It is supposed that she is gone to Horseneck, and probably may have changed her name as she went after a butcher named William Howard, (an apprentice to Mr. Boyart) who said he had married her the night before. She went off with the wife of one Lindsey, a Tanner, who is a servant, and it is said has inlisted in the Connecticut Forces, under General Woster. Whoever takes up and returns or secures the said woman servant, shall be entitled to the above reward, besides all reasonable charges. James Barrow. [*New York Journal*, June 29, 1775]

[157] Six Dollars Reward. A Dutch servant girl, named Christiana Beryon, had liberty on the 12th instant to go to Philadelphia, under pretence of getting a kinsman to purchase her time, and is not since returned; she took with her change of apparel, and appears well dressed in the German manner (except her cap and bonnet, which are country made); she is about 28 years of age, heavy made, in height rather above the middle size, has lost most of her single teeth, speaks broken English. Whoever takes up and secures the said servant, so that her master may get her again, shall receive the above reward, paid by David Cooper. [*New York Journal*, June 29, 1775]

[158] Run away on the 9th inst. June, from the subscriber, a Dutch Servant Woman, named Regina Burgmuller, 20 years of age, fair complexion, rather tall, large blue eyes, she frowns and is impudent if examined. Had on and took with her, a white short gown, one blue and white calicoe ditto, and one brown worsted damask ditto, a black bonnet with blue lining, a white silk handkerchief, with sundry other things. Whoever takes her up and commits her to the Work house, or brings her home, shall have Four Dollars Reward, paid by William Drewry. [*Pennsylvania Ledger*, July 1, 1775]

[159] Twenty Shillings Reward. Run away, last night, from the subscriber, an indented Irish servant girl, named Nancy Mackey, alias Munks; she is of a middle stature, light brown hair, has a remarkable sharp nose, is pitted with the smallpox, and speaks a little with the brogue in the pronunciation of some words; she had on, and took with her, a calicoe gown, a short gown of ditto, black Barcelona handkerchief, a striped lincey petticoat, a black rattinet quilted ditto, and new black taffaty bonnet; she will, very probably, endeavour to pass for a free woman, but as she had not yet served the time of her second indenture. Whoever secures said servant in any goal, and gives notice to her master, or brings her home, shall receive the above reward, and reasonable charges, paid by Robert Smith. [*Pennsylvania Gazette*, July 12, 1775]

[160] Thirty Pounds Reward. Run away from the subscriber, living in Newtown township, Gloucester county, West New Jersey, opposite Philadelphia, three Dutch servants; two on the 11th of May, man and wife, who have near 4 years to serve; the first named Henry Overkirker, about 5 feet high, thick set, has dark brown hair, is about 27 years old; had on, when he went away, a half-worn felt hat, a homespun cloth coloured jacket, with cuffs, black and white striped under jacket, white yarn stockings, and a pair of neat's leather shoes; his wife, Barbara, is about 18 years old, about 4 feet 10 inches high, has dark brown hair, black eyes, a round visage, and a remarkable high black mole on her upper lip; had on, when she went away, a check linen short gown, with an apron to it, a striped lincey petticoat, white yarn stockings, and a pair of

neat's leather shoes: It is supposed they have two uncles living in the province of Pennsylvania, known by the name of Lawrence Good and — Keller, and it is likely they will endeavour to find them out. The other on the 14th of June, named Jacob Crips, who has near 3 years to serve, is about 35 years old, about 5 feet 8 inches high, full faced, fair complexion, brown hair, well set, has 3 large scars proceeding from one place on his forehead, is a Butcher by trade, and inclinable to drink too much; had on, and took with him, a half-worn felt hat, a cloth coloured homespun jacket, with cuffs, a black and white thread underjacket, one pair of leather breeches, of an olive colour, very greasy, one pair of white yarn stockings, and a pair of neat's leather shoes. Whoever takes up and secures the said servants, so that their master may get them again, shall have the above reward, or Ten Pounds for each of them, and all reasonable charges, paid by Marmaduke Cooper. [*Pennsylvania Gazette*, July 12, 1775]

[161] Three Dollars Reward. Run away from the subscriber, living in Swanson street, Southwark, near the Sign of St. Patrick, an indented servant woman, named Jane Jackson, about 23 or 24 years of age; she is about 5 feet 1 or 2 inches high, a stout fat woman; came from Ireland; is an artful sly body; run away in March last, and was taken up at the Yellow Springs; it is likely she will change her name to that of Sally Hill, as she did before; had on, when she went away, a linen cap, a new shift, a new black quilt, lined with red serge, old shoes, with yellow buckles, a blue and white striped short gown, a good check apron, and a check handkerchief. Whoever secures the said servant in any of his Majesty's goals, so that her master may have her again, shall receive the above reward, and all reasonable charges, paid by Jacob Jones. [*Pennsylvania Gazette*, July 19, 1775]

[162] Five Pounds Reward. Run away from the Subscriber, the last evening, A native Irish Servant Man, calls himself John M'Gonnegall, 22 years of age, and 5 feet 7 or 8 inches high, thin visage, slim built, grey eyes, light brown hair and wears a club to it; a Barber by trade: had on and took with him, a blue cloth coat and jacket, buckskin breeches, almost new, three shirts, one brown

linen, a corded white jacket, striped linen ditto, a pair of red and white striped trowsers, a half worn castor hat, a new pair of black train shoes and plated buckles, both his legs sore, one very bad; came from Colerain the last fall; it is thought that the same night he run away he was seen near John Tomlinson's place, on the road leading from Wilmington to Lancaster, in company with another servant man of mine who run away two nights before, (and is now advertised in the papers) and an English woman who came in this spring with Benjamin Taylor, and now a servant to Ellis Newlin of said county, and it is likely that one of the men and woman may pass for man and wife, if they do not get tired of her and turn her adrift. She is about 21 yeas of age, red faced, low stature and thick built, loves strong drink, and is a great talker, had on, a white diaper bonnet, old patched reddish colour'd gown, red & blue strip'd linsey petticoat, a pair of old whitish coloured cloth shoes with metal buckles. Any person apprehending the said John M'Gonnegall, so that his master shall get him again, shall receive the above reward, if out of this county, and if in this county, Five Shillings over and above what the law allows; and any person that will apprehend the above described woman, so that her master shall get her again, if out of this county, Thirty Shillings, and if within the county, what the law allows. All persons are desired to discover the above Runaways, and as well all other such Runaways, otherwise there will be no such thing as keeping a Servant. William Brobson. Ellis Newlin. [*Pennsylvania Mercury and Universal Advertiser*, July 21, 1775]

[163] Run away from the subscriber in Charles City, last May, a likely young negro wench named Nanny, the property of Charles Carter, esq; of Corotoman; she is of a yellowish complexion, slender made and is fond of dress. She had on, and took with her, a calico waistcoat and petticoat, one blue plains ditto, and sundry other apparel. She went off with a free negro fellow, who pretends being a doctor, commonly wears a laced hat, and is about 6 feet high; he has been guilty of stealing several horses from this county, for which he is fled, and, if taken, will certainly receive a punishment due to the offence. Whoever brings the said wench to me at Shirley shall have 3 l. reward, or 4 s. if secured so that she may be had

again, and all reasonable expenses, paid by John Currell. [Purdie's *Virginia Gazette*, July 21, 1775]

[164] Committed to the gaol of Buckingham a negro woman, about 4 feet 8 inches high, affects that she cannot speak her master's name, though says her name is Chloe. She is dressed with a blue and white Swanskin petticoat, oznabrig shirt, and striped homespun jacket. She was born in Africa, and appears to be about 40 years of age. The owner is desired to pay prison charges, and take her out. John Cox, gaoler. [Pinkney's *Virginia Gazette*, July 27, 1775]

[165] Twenty Shillings Reward. Went away a few days ago, from her master, in Newtown, Bucks County, an Irish servant woman named Catherine Magill, well set, about five feet five or six inches high, twenty-six or twenty-seven years of age; had on and took with her, two long gowns, one of straw coloured stuff and the other of a green and white stuff, an India calico short gown, a short white silk cloak trimmed with ermine, a high crown blue bonnet and a small black bonnet: She writes a remarkable good hand, and says her father was a gauger in some part of Ireland. Whoever takes up the said servant, and delivers her either to Mr. Whitehead, Work-house keeper, in Philadelphia, or to Mr. John Anderson, Gaol keeper, in Trenton, shall receive from them the above Reward, and all reasonable charges.

N. B. All persons are forbid to harbour the said servant at their peril; but if any should be inclinable to purchase her time, they may have, by applying to Mr. Charles Bessonett in Bristol, her indentures assigned over for a small consideration. [*Pennsylvania Packet*, July 31, 1775]

[166] Two Dollars Reward. Run away, last Sunday night, from the subscriber, living near the New market, in Second street, an indented English servant girl, named Betsey Smith, about 17 years of age, a little pitted with the smallpox, and had six toes on one foot; had on, when she went away, an old red sattin petticoat, lined with white muslin, a white corded short gown, black bonnet, and new leather shoes. Jacob Bunner. [*Pennsylvania Gazette*, August 9, 1775]

[167] Run away, in the night of the 19th instant, from the subscriber, in Yorktown, an Irish servant girl, named Margaret Thornton, about 19 years of age, about 5 feet 2 inches high, red hair, strong built, her face and arms much freckled: Had on, and took with her, a brownish poplin gown, ruffled, a black quilted petticoat, greenish lining, a dark brown lincey petticoat, a silk handkerchief, two shifts, one white apron, one check ditto, an old black silk cloak, two pair of old white stockings, a pair of black everlasting shoes, two calicoe short gowns, and an old single white handkerchief. Whoever takes up said servant girl, and secures her, so that her master may get her again, shall receive Eight Dollars reward, paid by Ephraim Penington. [*Pennsylvania Gazette*, August 9, 1775]

[168] Four Dollars Reward. Ran away on Tuesday the 18th inst. (July) from the subscriber, living in New Providence Township, Philadelphia County, an English servant Girl named Ann Owen, about twenty-two years of age, fair hair turned high up; had on a light green gown, white apron, bonnet, and cloth shoes. Whoever takes up and secures said servant so that her master may have her again, shall be paid the above Reward, by Richard Swanwick. [*Pennsylvania Packet*, August 14, 1775]

[169] Twenty Shillings Reward. Run away, last Saturday, from the subscriber, living in Callowhill street, the corner of Water street, a Negroe Woman, named Rachel, about 30 years of age, and has a remarkable austere countenance. She had on, and took with her, a black bonnet, furniture check petticoat, striped short gown, check apron, a coloured handkerchief, a new Irish linen shirt not quite made, green silk umbrella almost new, and a hymn book with the subscribers name in it. Whoever secures said woman, so that her mistress gets her again, shall have the above reward. Mary Deklyn. [*Pennsylvania Gazette*, August 23, 1775]

[170] Six Pence Reward Ran away from the subscriber yesterday, the 2th inst. an apprentice girl named Mary Patterson, about nineteen years of age, rather tall and slender, of a swarthy complexion, a little marked with the smallpox, has a very bold look, and is ignorant and saucy. She had on, and took with her, an old white

bonnet, an old calico blue and yellow sprig gown, and an old blue quilt petticoat. Whoever apprehends the above apprentice, and secures her in any of his Majesty's jails so that her master may have her again, shall receive the above reward and no charges. Philip Fullan, Market street. [*Pennsylvania Gazette*, August 30, 1775]

[171] Twenty Dollars Reward. Run away from the subscriber, living on Elk Ridge, in Anne Arundel county, Maryland, the 18th of July last, two indented Irish servants, viz. John Hays, a shoemaker, about 25 years of age, 5 feet 10 inches high, with dark brown hair; had on, and took with him, a half worn fan tail hat, brown broadcloth coat, the cape faced with redish coloured velvet, with metal buttons, a red waistcoat, two white shirts, one ozenbrigs ditto, a white neckcloth, country linen trowsers, black and white yarn hose, country shoes, and plated buckles. Eleanor Hays, 18 years of age, about 5 feet 3 or 4 inches high, slender made, thin visage, and speaks much on the brogue, black hair, and is much freckled; had on a red camblet gown, a lincey petticoat, one red ditto, one white shift, one brown ditto, check apron, one brown ditto, country made shoes, and white hose. Whoever takes up said servants, and secures them in any goal, so that their master may get them again, shall have the above reward, or Half for either of them, and reasonable charges, if brought home, paid by Joseph Hobbs, senior.

N. B. He has a wallet and some shoemaker's tools with him it is probable that he may alter his name and change his clothes; all masters of vessels are forbid carrying them off, at their peril. [*Pennsylvania Gazette*, August 30, 1775]

[172] Four Dollars Reward. Ran away on Thursday evening, the 3d inst. from the subscriber, a Dutch servant girl named Maria Catherine Mamro, eighteen years of age, black hair, a scar on one of her cheek bones, dark complexion, bobs in her ears, and low in stature; had on when she went away, a broad striped blue and white cotton lincey petticoat, a callico short gown, black silk bonnet; she took with her a blue and white narrow striped short gown and petticoat, a garnet coloured camblet skirt, a dark ground callico ditto, and sundry other cloaths: She goes by the name of Caty,

and supposed to be gone with one Conrad Konigsfeld to Mr. Wistar's Glass house in the Jerseys. Whoever secures said servant so that her master may have her again, shall be entitled to the above Reward. Richard Footman. [*Pennsylvania Packet*, September 4, 1775]

[173] Run away, on the 26th of August last, from the subscriber, an Irish servant girl, named Ann Skilling, middle sized, came in the ship Charlotte, Captain Edgar, has red hair, full faced, fresh complexion, stoop shoulders, and speaks the Scotch dialect a little; had on, when she went off, a light blue stuff gown. As it is supposed she is gone with some of the passengers, it is hoped no person will harbour her. Whoever brings her to Mr. Whitehead, at the Workhouse, shall receive Fifteen Shillings reward, paid by Robert Gordon Hall. [*Pennsylvania Gazette*, September 6, 1775]

[174] Run away, on the 8th day of the 8th month last, from the subscriber, living in Lampeter township, Lancaster county, a native Irish girl, named Catherine Kennedy, a fresh, lusty like girl, with black hair; which said she was with child to a certain Henry McGlaughlin, an hired servant with the subscriber, and said McGlaughlin went away in the night time of the night before her; it appears that she told some of the family, that she would follow him go where he would, till she would find him. Said servant took with her striped lincey petticoats, a calicoe short gown, check apron, with several other clothes. Whoever takes up said servant, and brings her to her master, shall have Five Shillings reward, and their labour for their pains. James Smith. [*Pennsylvania Gazette*, September 20, 1775]

[175] Forty Shillings Reward. Run from the subscriber, on Sunday night, the 10th of September, 1775, an English servant woman, has been in the country about 8 or 9 years, she was sold for having a mulatto bastard; she is a well set woman, about 5 feet 3 or 4 inches high, had dark coloured hair, her name is Eleanor Davis, and she has three different suits of clothes to wear; she has a dark striped calicoe gown, a red and white calicoe ditto, a short white sack and petticoat, a pale blue silk bonnet, shoes and stockings.

Whoever takes up said servant, shall have the above reward, and all reasonable charges, paid by James Buller, Queen's Town, Queen Anne's county.

N. B. She went away in company with an Irish servant man of Francis Hall, of the same county; the man talks much on the Irish dialect, and has dark blue grey clothes. [*Pennsylvania Gazette*, September 27, 1775]

[176] Twenty Shillings Reward. Run away from the subscriber, in Bristol township, Philadelphia county, on the 20th of this instant September, an Irish servant Girl, named Elizabeth McConegal, about 20 years of age, of a dark complexion, much pitted with the smallpox, of a short chunky stature, speaks plain English, had on, and took with her, two lincey petticoats, one striped the other plain, a coarse tow shift, two short gowns, one striped homespun the other calicoe, a pair of calfskin shoes, with plain metal buckles, a black silk bonnet, with red lining, a spotted red and white handkerchief, and one single Kenton ditto, two homespun aprons, one white tow the other check, and one fine check ditto, with a running string. Whoever will secure said servant in any of his Majesty's goals, and sends word to her master, also that he may have her again, shall be intitled to the above reward, and reasonable charges, if brought home, paid by Caleb Armitage. [*Pennsylvania Gazette*, September 27, 1775]

[177] Six Dollars Reward. Run away on the 25th Instant, from the Subscriber, living in Water-Street, between Lombard-Street and South-Street, an Irish Servant Woman, named Frances Scot, aged about 30 years. She is a well set Woman, about five feet five inches high, and has dark coloured hair. Had on and took with her, when she went away, a check short gown, a black quilt, a lace cap with a white ribbon round it, new leather shoes with plated buckles in them, white thread stockings, two long gowns one a reddish sprig, the other a Pompadore poplin, a black hat full trim'd, and a pair of stuff shoes almost new, with several other things not known. It is supposed she will change her name. Whoever takes up the said Servant, and secures her so as her Master may have her again, shall have the above Reward and reasonable charges paid by Cornelius Hillman. [*Pennsylvania Ledger*, September 30, 1775]

[178] Ran away from the Subscriber on the 12th Instant, a Negro Girl about 17 or 18 Years old, thick set, speaks good English, has a Scar across her Nose and another Scar on the top of one Foot occasioned by a burn: Had on a tow Shift, a striped woolen Petticoat, and a brown Gown. Whoever will return her to me in Groton, shall have Two Dollars Reward, and all necessary Charges paid by Mortemore Stodder. [*New London Gazette*, October 6, 1775]

[179] Ran away from the Subscriber, the 6th Instant, a Girl named Elisabeth Wright, midling size, brownish Hair, about 17 Years old; she carried away two Gowns, one brown over shot with red, white and blue, and a linnen Ditto with large blue Streaks in the Chain, and over shot in the filling. Whoever will return her to Jonah Strickland, in Chatham, shall have six pence Reward. All Persons are forbid to harbour her on Penalty of the Law. [*New London Gazette*, October 13, 1775]

[180] Lost from the subscriber, living on Raccoon creek, in Woolwich township, Gloucester county, West New-Jersey, in the night between the 9th and 10th of this instant October, an indented female child; her name is Polly Murphy, very near 5 years of age, pretty tall for her age, of a fair complexion, has ruddy cheeks, grey eyes, light hair, and a small scar on her forehead; had on an almost new homespun lincey petticoat, with red, brown and yellow stripes, turned up round-about, a red ragged woollen short gown, and a coarse ozenbrigs shift. It is supposed she has been taken away by her parents, who stayed that night with the subscriber, and with the child disappeared in the morning. The father's name is Henry Scharff, has a lean face and thin hair, and had on an old worn out blue coat; the mother is a lusty, hearty woman, of a fair complexion, has thick lips, and black hair, and is big with child. Whoever takes up the said persons with the above described child, and secures them, so that the subscribers may have the child again, and the parents convicted of the theft, shall have five pounds reward, or for the child alone three pounds, and all reasonable charges paid by Andrew Mintz. [*Pennsylvania Gazette*, October 18, 1775]

[181] Two Dollars Reward. Ran away (a second time) on Tuesday morning, the 17th inst. (October) from a house in Water-street, an Irish servant girl named Ann Skilling; middle sized, full face, fresh complexion, red hair, stern looking brows, stoop shoulders, has an aukward way of walking, wears a light blue stuff gown; as she stole away her cloaths when she first ran away, and did not bring them back, she may change her apparel. Any person or persons, harbouring said run-away after this notice, will be prosecuted as the law directs. Whoever secures her and lodges her in the Work-house, shall have the above Reward, paid by Robert G. Hall. [*Pennsylvania Packet*, October 30, 1775]

[182] Five Pounds Reward. Run away from the subscriber, on the night of 21st inst. a man and woman, convicts, viz. William Manly, a well made man, 5 feet 8 inches high, 25 or 30 years of age, with black hair cut short, of a surly bad countenance, is a labourer, and understands horses; had on, when he went away, a short blue coat, about half worn, and either a light coloured spotted jean, or a brown cloth jacket, flannel drawers, strong self grey knit stockings, and strong English made shoes; is an impudent active fellow, and speaks the North of England dialect. Anne Wilson, who calls herself the aforesaid Manly's wife, is a thin looking woman, 5 feet 2 inches high, about 40 or 45 years of age, speaks the same dialect as Manly, and is in a tolerable good working dress. Whoever takes up and secures the above convicts, so that I get them again, shall receive, if taken in this province, Forty Shillings for the man, and Twenty Shillings for the woman; and if takes up out of this province, Three Pounds for the man, and Two Pounds for the woman. They stole, and took with them, a frying pan, a copper tea kettle, several Irish linen shirts, and sundry provisions, &c. There is reason to believe they have got a false pass, and are making for Philadelphia; they were seen near Queen's Town, in Queen Anne's county, on Sunday, the 22d instant, about noon, and at Warwick, in Caecil county, on Wednesday morning following. James Braddock. [*Pennsylvania Gazette*, November 8, 1775]

[183] Four Dollars Reward. Run away, in the night of the 12th of this instant November, from the subscriber, in Bethel township,

Chester county, a native Irish servant woman named Mary Cortney, aged about 25 years, says she has a husband in the army at Boston, has full grey eyes, and black hair, a short and chunky body; had on and took with her, when she went away, two long gowns, one striped calicoe, patched, the other good, a black silk hat, a brown skirt, and a striped flannel petticoat, one pair of shoes, and a pair of channel pumps, one check apron, blue stockings, and a claret coloured cloak with a cap, and a check bag to carry her things. Whoever secures said servant, so as her master may have her again, shall have the above reward, and reasonable charges paid by Joseph Larkin. [*Pennsylvania Gazette*, November 13, 1775]

[184] Six Dollars Reward. Run away from the subscriber, living in Pine street, between Second and Third streets, an Irish servant girl, named Elizabeth Cleland, about 17 years of age, about 5 feet high, has black hair and black eyes, is very much marked with the smallpox; had on, and took with her, when she went away, a dark cross barred camblettee gown, a halfthick blue petticoat, patched before, a dark calimancoe ditto, lined with red shaloon, 1 sheeting shift, and 1 fine ozenbrigs ditto, almost new, 2 pair of shoes, 2 bonnets, one black, the other white, 1 Barcelona handkerchief, 1 India flag ditto, 1 blue and white ditto, and 1 pale red ditto, a sett of light blue small beads, a blue shag cloak, a short gown, with a purple running sprig, a pair of locket buttons, and a Lisbon needle case, with several other things unknown. Whoever takes up and secures said servant, so that her mistress may have her again, shall have the above reward, and reasonable charges, paid by Elizabeth Robertson. [*Pennsylvania Gazette,* November 15, 1775]

[185] Ran away from the Subscriber, in Newcastle County, on the 14th instant, (November) a servant woman named Catharine Carr, about 22 years of age, a middle sized person; had with her when she went away, a gown of stamped linen, a short ditto of purple calico, two striped lincey petticoats, a red skirt, and a black bonnet. Whoever takes up said servant woman, shall have Six Pence Reward, and no more, paid by William Patterson. [*Pennsylvania Packet*, December 18, 1775]

1776

[186] Run away from the subscriber, living in Franconia township, Philadelphia county, an English servant maid, named Mary Stuart, has light brown hair, grey eyes, and is about 5 feet two inches high; had on, when she went away, a dark brown gown, a black, white, and red calicoe short gown, three striped lincey petticoats, two of them black and white, a black bonnet, old linen apron, two tow aprons, a dark striped silk handkerchief, and a white flowered lawn ditto, old blue stockings, footed with black, good strong new shoes, with white metal buckles. Whoever secures said servant, so as her master may have her again, shall have Forty Shillings reward, and reasonable charges, paid by George Chrisman. [*Pennsylvania Gazette*, January 10, 1776]

[187] Eight Dollars Reward. Ran away last night from the subscriber, living at the corner of Water and Walnut streets, a Dutch servant woman named Clara Ingerbloed; she appears to be about 40 years of age, a short chunky woman, very talkative; had on and took with her, a dark purple and white cotton long gown, a half worn blue quilted petticoat, a striped lincey jacket, three striped lincey petticoats, one scarlet halfthick ditto, two pair of white yarn, and one pair of blue worsted stockings with white clocks, a pair of half worn shoes, and a pair of pumps almost new, two good check aprons, one good white ditto, a coarser white ditto, and an oznabrigs one quite new, three shifts with open sleeves and loose sleeves to pin on, two bonnets of black peelong, and a dove

coloured fine camblet long cloak faced down before with tammy nearly the same colour. 'Tis supposed she is gone off with a servant man (named Frederick Dickmire) belonging to Nicholas Rittenhouse, Miller, near Germantown. Whoever takes up and secures said servant woman, so that her master may have her again, shall receive the above Reward, and reasonable charges, paid by William Forbes. [*Pennsylvania Packet*, January 15, 1776]

[188] Two Dollars Reward. Ran away from the subscriber, an English servant girl named Amelia Way, about five feet two or three inches high, middling thick, has light coloured hair, a little on the dark complexion; had on and took with her when she went away, an old English lincey petticoat, a bird-eye yellowish stuff ditto, a brown camblet ditto, a Mecklenburg redish ground short gown, green flower much faded, a purple and white India ditto, a pair of leather stays, a pair of leather high-heeled shoes, an old red short cloak, and a black silk bonnet; talks in the West country dialect, and stoops forward in her walk; was seen crossing Rudolph's Ferry, in company with a young lad about sixteen or seventeen years of age. Whoever secures said servant so that her mistress may have her again, shall be entitled to the above Reward, and reasonable charges, paid by Mary Magee. [*Pennsylvania Packet*, January 15, 1776]

[189] One Dollar Reward. Run away in the night of the 15th inst. from the Subscriber, living in Arch street, Philadelphia, an English servant girl, named Ann Watson, about five feet high, has dark hair, a pale complexion, and marked with the smallpox; had on when she went away a dark brown stuff gown, a black quilt, check apron, red cloak, and black hat, wears a Queen's nightcap, made of plain linen; looks very innocent, but is given to drink. Whoever secures said servant, so that her master may get her again, shall have the above reward, and reasonable charges, paid by Thomas Dowman. [*Pennsylvania Gazette*, January 17, 1776]

[190] Four Dollars Reward. Ran away from the subscriber, living in Salisbury township, Lancaster county, on the second day of second month, 1776, a servant woman, named Margaret Collands, about 30 years of age, of a dark complexion, has black hair, is

about 5 feet high, she stole and took with her two shifts and some caps, a red, white and yellow striped cotton and worsted gown, a yellow and brown striped linsey petticoat, an old yellow quilt, a half worn blue and brown petticoat, a reddish coloured worsted bonnet, a blue handkerchief with white spots, a lincey check apron, high heeled shoes, and blue stockings with white feet and tops. Whoever takes up the said servant, and secures her, so that her master may have her again, shall have the above reward, and reasonable charges, paid by William Chamberlain, or by Robert Wood, Parchment maker, in Fifth street, Philadelphia. [*Pennsylvania Gazette*, February 14, 1776]

[191] Forty Shillings Reward. Run Away, last Thursday evening, from the subscriber, living in Second street, near Market street, a Negroe woman, named Hannah, about 21 years old, a stout made, hearty girl, full faced, but rather down countenance, scars on her cheeks (the marks of her tribe in Guinea) had only her work clothes on, being a green baize short gown, striped lincey petticoat, an old pair of mens shoes, and stockings, a plain linen cap. Whoever will bring said Negroe women to her master, shall have the above reward, and reasonable charges. Robert Coupar. It is supposed that she is lurking in town, as she has been seen since she went off. [*Pennsylvania Gazette*, February 21, 1776]

[192] Ran-away from the Subscriber, on the 26th ult. a Negro Girl named Cloe, had on a short Wrapper, red and blue mixt, a white flannel Shift, a striped Petticoat, black and white, work'd with Crewel, she is thick set, about 16 or 17 Years old, had a Scar on her Foot, occasioned by a Burn, also a Scar on her Nose and another on her Ear. Whoever will take her up and return her to me shall have two Dollars Reward. Mortimer Stodder. [*Connecticut Gazette*, February 23, 1776]

[193] Four Dollars Reward. Ran Away from the subscriber, living in Swanson street, Southwark, near the sign of St. Patrick, an indented servant woman named Jane Jackson, 23 or 24 years old, 5 feet 1 or 2 inches high, she is a stout fat woman, came from Ireland about the 27th of July 1774, in Capt. M'Clenaghan's ship; she is an artful, sly body, and perhaps may pass for a married

woman, as she has got a certificate with her belonging to Susanna Walsh: Had on when she went away, a blue and red striped short gown, a new black quilt with red lining, a check apron, old shoes and stockings, two or three check handkerchiefs, and sundry other things. Whoever takes up, and secures the said servant in any of his Majesty's gaols, so that the subscriber may have her again, shall have the above Reward and all reasonable charges, paid by Jacob Jones. [*Pennsylvania Packet*, February 25, 1776]

[194] Two Dollars Reward. Run away, on Friday, the 9th of February last, from the subscriber, in Bristol township, Philadelphia county, a Dutch servant woman, named Agnes Hartman, about 25 years of age, very lusty, 5 feet 2 or 3 inches high, light hair, dark complexion, much pitted with the smallpox; took with her one cotton chintz gown, several bed gowns, lincey petticoats and Dutch clothes. Whoever will bring said servant to her master shall have the above reward, paid by John Moor, or John Hay. [*Pennsylvania Gazette*, March 6, 1776]

[195] Ten Pounds Reward. Run away, on the 12th of March, 1776, from the subscriber, living in Water street, near Market street, Philadelphia, the following servants, viz. Frederick Brick, a German, born in the country of Hesse, about 29 years of age, about 5 feet high, by trade a taylor, has brownish hair, intermixed with grey, speaks good Hollandish and German, and very quick; he is very apt to get drunk, and very unruly when so; Had on and took with him, when he went away, a blue cloth coat, waistcoat and breeches of blue hair plush, a grey nap surtout, new shoes, one white and three check shirts, a new raccoon hat, a pair of ribbed and a pair of plain worsted stockings. Magdalene Brick (his wife) born in the country of Wertenberg, in Germany, she is remarkably round shouldered, her fingers and thumbs are all crooked, has sandy hair, and of a pale complexion: Took with her a brown damask gown, and black petticoat with white flowers. They took with them a small female child, about six months old, and were seen about 35 miles from Philadelphia on the Bethlehem road. It is supposed they are gone towards Shamokin, as the man ran away once before, and was taken up near Fort Augusta. Whoever takes

up the above described servants, and secures them in any goal, and acquaints the subscriber thereof, shall receive the above reward, paid by William Hembel. [*Pennsylvania Gazette*, March 27, 1776]

[196] A Scotch Girl, named Jane Forbes, about 20 years of age, ran away from the subscriber, in Arch street, Philadelphia, a round full face, with high cheek bones, is pitted with the smallpox, had black eyes, and a soft inarticulate voice, speaks much in the Scotch dialect, has the appearance of great good humour, and affects a modest downcast look; her dress was a cloth coloured pelong bonnet, lined with pale blue mantua, light coloured cloth cloak, with a hood and gimp, broad striped ribbon round her neck, white kenting handkerchief, brown and yellow camblettee gown, blue stuff quilted petticoat, lined with blue baize, and a pale green and white striped lincey jacket and petticoat. Twenty Shillings will be paid to any person who secures her in any goal, within 20 miles of Philadelphia, and Forty Shillings if at a greater distance, together with all reasonable Charges. Richard Wells. [*Pennsylvania Gazette*, April 3, 1776]

[197] Ran Away, lately, from the Subscriber's plantation, on Charlestown Neck, a Negro Wench, named Letitia, who is about 18 years of age, middle sized, with a scar in one cheek; and then had on a purple and white striped camblet gown, and brown worsted petticoat, and formerly belonged to George Jackson, in Ponpon, where she has several relations, and a numerous acquaintance, among whom it is suspected, she is harboured. The above negro was born in this Province, is very intelligent, and well known in Charlestown. Any person apprehending and delivering the said negro to the Warden of the Work house, or to the keeper of any of the country gaols, shall be entitled to a reward of Ten Pounds, besides all lawful charges; and those who carry her over ferries, or conceal her, may depend on the severest prosecution. Robert Williams, jun. [*South Carolina and American General Gazette*, April 17, 1776]

[198] Run away, on the night of the 6th day of April instant, from the subscriber, in Newgarden township, Chester county, an Irish servant woman, named Anne Crage, about 40 years of age, red

faced, and sandy hair; had on, when she went away, an old quilt and a black under petticoat, an old calicoe bedgown, a spotted blue and white handkerchief, and supposed to have taken a red map ditto with her, had neither shoes nor stockings; she was brought from Philadelphia by one Steel, she says she has a husband, called John Crage. Whoever takes up said servant, and brings her to her master, or secures her in any goal, so that her master may have her again, shall have Twenty Shillings reward, and reasonable charges, paid by Stephen Anderson. [*Pennsylvania Gazette*, April 17, 1776]

[199] Forty Shillings Reward. Run away last night, from the subscribers, living near Brandywine Bridge, two Irish servant women, one named Margaret Ferguson, about 40 years of age, tall and lusty, stoop shouldered, with short light or sandy coloured hair. The other named Mary Caulfield, 24 years of age, of low stature, but thick and strongly built, with black or dark brown hair; had on, and took with them, one camblet riding habit, faced with blue peelong, one old taffaty gown, of a straw colour, one other cotton and linen gown, of a light green colour, two calicoe and one lincey short gown, 3 striped lincey petticoats, a black quilt, a grey coating cloak, without a cape, each a black bonnet, one low the other high heeled shoes, &c. Any person securing the said servants, so that their masters may have them again, shall be entitled to the above reward, and reasonable charges, paid by William Starr, and Joseph Tatnall. [*Pennsylvania Gazette*, April 24, 1776]

[200] Four Dollars Reward. Run away from the subscriber, living in Hanover township, Lancaster county, on the 18th of March past, a servant Girl, about 13 or 14 years of age, of a brown complexion, lightish brown short hair; had on, when she went away, a short gown and petticoat, made of striped lincey, the stripes are pale green and white, the petticoat has 3 small red stripes in it, they are far asunder; she is supposed to be taken off by her father and mother, who live in Philadelphia; her father's name is John Cogdal, and the girl's name Sidney Cogdal, which is also her mother's name. This is the second time of her running away. Whoever takes up said servant, and brings her home, or secures her, so that her master may have her again, shall have the above reward, and reasonable charges, paid by James Rippeth. [*Pennsylvania Gazette*, May 1, 1776]

[201] Run away from the subscriber in Albemarle, the 1st of this instant (May) a very likely light mulatto woman named Bess, about 24 years old, thin visaged, has a small scar on her left elbow, occasioned by a burn, and it is probable will endeavour to pass for a free woman. She carried off with her a number of clothes, among them two gowns, one striped with blue, the other with copperas and blue, three cotton and three linen shifts, four petticoats, two striped with blue, the other two with copperas, a pair of high-heeled leather shoes, a pair of fine thread stockings, a white cotton bonnet, and one of black silk. Whoever conveys the said slave to me, or secures her so that I get her again, shall have 20 s. reward, besides what the law allows. John Strange. [Purdie's *Virginia Gazette*, May 24, 1776]

[202] Ran away from the subscriber, on Wednesday last, the 29th ult. an Irish servant woman, named Sarah Clark, about twenty-five years of age, and of a very dark complexion. Had on, when she went away, a dark calico gown, check apron, a black calamanco skirt, a blue and white check handkerchief, and a black silk bonnet. Whoever takes up the said servant, and secures her so that her master gets her again, shall have Twenty Shillings reward, and reasonable charges. William Smith. [*Pennsylvania Evening Post*, June 1, 1776]

[203] Eight Dollars Reward. Run away the 2d inst. from the subscriber, living in Bethel township, Chester county, a Dutch servant lad named Hans Henry Bartram, about 19 years of age, 5 feet 7 or 8 inches high, speaks broken English, and has brown hair; had on, when he went away, a snuff coloured cloth home made, one pair of good buckskin breeches, one pair of blue ribbed stockings, old shoes, a new tow shirt, and felt hat. Also an Irish servant woman, named Mary Cartney, about 25 years of age; she had on a calicoe gown and check apron, a black silk hat, two pair of yarn stockings, and good shoes. Whoever secures the said servants, so that their master may get them again, shall have the above reward, or Five Dollars for the lad, and Three Dollars for the woman, with reasonable charges, paid by Joseph Larkin. [*Pennsylvania Gazette*, June 5, 1776]

[204] Run away from the Subscriber, on the 24th Ult. a likely Negro Girl about 16 Years of Age, named Esther, formerly the Property of Mr. Miles King of Hampton. She has lost a Joint of one of her Fingers of her right Hand, had on a blue Plains Jacket, and a Negro Cotton Coat. I will give 20 s. if she is taken up within 20 Miles of this City, and if at a greater Distance 40 s. and delivered to me in Williamsburg. John Shiphard. [Dixon & Hunter's *Virginia Gazette*, June 8, 1776]

[205] Four Dollars Reward. Run away from the subscriber, June 18, 1776, a servant Girl, named Mary Allen, of middle size, straight and well made, freckled in the face and arms, grey eyes, dark brown hair, a gauze cap, raised with a roller, an old straw hat, black mittens on her arms, a calicoe short gown, a dirty coloured lincey petticoat, a red under ditto, high heeled calf skin shoes, white cotton stockings; says she was born in England, and brought to Cecil county, Maryland, at 12 years of age, where she served her time; she afterwards went to Philadelphia and was put in goal on suspicion, but nothing proved against her, and she was sold to the subscriber for her cost. Whoever secures said servant in any goal, shall have the above reward, and reasonable charges, if brought to Joseph Park, in Sadsbury township, Chester county. [*Pennsylvania Gazette*, June 26, 1776]

[206] Run away from the subscriber, an Irish servant Girl, named Elizabeth Nangel, about 19 years of age, of a fair complexion, light brown hair, remarkable short, and a negrofied nose; she speaks on the Irish dialect; had on, and took with her, a black bonnet, a cap with edging round it, a calicoe short gown, two striped lincey petticoats, check apron, two shifts, a pair of calfskin pumps, with carved Pinchbeck buckles all new. Whoever takes her up, and secures her, so that her master may get her again, shall receive the reward of Eight Dollars, and reasonable charges, paid by Abel Rees. [*Pennsylvania Gazette*, July 3, 1776]

[207] Eight Dollars Reward. Run away the 19th of June, in the morning, from the subscriber, Mary Smith, a Scotch servant, between 17 and 18 years old, about 5 feet 4 or 5 inches high, her right shoulder considerable higher than the left, dark hair; had on

Mary Smith, "a Scotch servant, between 17 and 18 years old" with "her right shoulder considerably higher than the left" wears "a homespun coat, a blue and white striped short gown, black bonnet, a pair of leather pumps almost new, yellow buckles," a "check apron," and carries a "red cloak." See advertisement 207 from the *New York Journal*, July 4, 1776. Illustration by Eric H. Schnitzer.

when she went away, a homespun coat, a blue and white striped short gown, black bonnet, a pair of leather pumps almost new, yellow buckles, took with her one callico long gown, purple and white, one short check gown, three check aprons, two shifts, three white handkerchiefs, one red cloak. Whoever apprehends the above runaway, and secures her in gaol, so that I may have her again, shall receive the above reward from me. Henry Walkeys.

N. B. Tis supposed the above runaway is gone towards Philadelphia. [*New York Journal*, July 4, 1776]

[208] Three Dollars Reward. Run away from the subscriber, living in Radnor township, Chester county, on the 12th of this instant July, an Irish indented servant maid, named Catherine Caisey, a chunky fat lump, broad faced, a down look, her hair cut short round her head, about 5 feet 2 inches high; had on, when she went away, a striped lincey short gown and petticoat, of black and white colour. Whoever takes up and secures the above described maid, shall have the above reward, and reasonable charges, paid by Mr. Ogden, at the Middle Ferry, or by James Hunter.

N. B. It is judged she is lurking about the Barracks of Philadelphia, or somewhere about town. [*Pennsylvania Gazette*, July 17, 1776]

[209] Two Dollars Reward. Run away from the subscriber, the 15th of May last, a Negroe Wench, named Violet, about 27 years of age, she is pretty lusty and fat, she has lived some time with Anthony Hall, tavernkeeper; had on, when she went away, a homespun lincey petticoat, and a coarse green baize short gown; lost one of her under fore teeth, her two thumbs are remarkably round, short and stumpy; she has been seen about the lower part of the city and Society Hill. Whoever will take up said Negroe Wench, and secure her in the Workhouse, or bring her home, shall have the above reward, and reasonable charges, paid by Christopher Pechin. [*Pennsylvania Gazette*, July 24, 1776]

[210] Ten Pounds Reward. Ran away from the subscriber's plantation, in Sussex County, on Delaware, on the 8th day of April, 1775, a Negro wench named Sarah, about twenty years of age, well made, and about five feet or six inches high, with tolerable thick

lips and a down look; had remarkable long wool on her head for a Negro, which she usually tied on the top: Had on and took with her, sundry good homemade cloaths. The above Reward will be paid to any person who will deliver the said wench to the subscriber, living in Snow hill Town, Worcester County, Maryland, or to Burton Waples, living in Sussex County aforesaid, or Eight Pounds if confined in any gaol, so that the subscriber may get her again, with all reasonable charges paid by Nathaniel Waples.

N. B. It is supposed she left the country aforesaid about the latter end of October or the first of November last, with a Negro fellow named Peter, belonging to Thomas Robinson, of the county aforesaid, who ran away about that time: He is about twenty years of age, a thick, well set fellow, and about five feet six inches high; it is imagined he had about 6 or 8l. Cash, and well cloathed: He has remarkable hairy temple locks, unless cut off by shaving. It is well known that the said wench was harboured and kept by the fellow aforesaid during the above interval, and it was supposed she was with child by said fellow when she ran away, and that they will try to pass for free Negroes and as husband and wife. The woman can read. [*Pennsylvania Packet*, July 22, 1776]

[211] Run away on the 19th of May last, a servant Girl, named Anne Munro, late from Scotland, aged about 18 years, low of stature, fair complexion, brown hair, and supposed to be with child; she had on, when she went away, a green baize short gown, striped lincey petticoat, tow apron, and check handkerchief. Whoever will secure the said Anne Munro in the Goal or Workhouse in Philadelphia, or bring her to the subscriber, in the Manor of Mooreland, Philadelphia county, shall be paid Twenty Shillings, with reasonable charges, by Edward Duffield. [*Pennsylvania Gazette*, July 24, 1776]

[212] Run away from the subscriber, this morning, an Irish servant maid, named Margaret Owings, a fat, lusty fresh coloured person, about 5 feet 6 inches high, dark hair and grey eyes; had on, and took with her, a calicoe gown, brown cloth petticoat, green bonnet, a coarse linen apron, and an old check ditto, one pair high heeled shoes, one pair low heeled ditto, and a cross barred cotton and kenting handkerchief. Whoever apprehends said maid, and

secures her, so that she may be had again, shall have Thirty Shillings reward, paid by Joseph Bentley. [*Pennsylvania Gazette*, July 24, 1776]

[213] Four Dollars Reward. Ran away from the subscriber, living at Duck Creek Cross Roads, in Kent County on Delaware, on the 8th of May last, an Irish servant girl named Elizabeth Buckly, about twenty-seven years of age, five feet six or seven inches high, much marked with the small-pox, fair hair and complexion, long nose, a good set of teeth, grey eyes, and was born in Corke; had on and took with her, a long purple calico gown, two striped linen short gowns and one lincey ditto, two old black quilts, two lincey petticoats, one flowered lawn apron, one old check ditto, a black bonnet with lace round the edge, a pair of leather shoes and plated buckles, and a red cloth cloak with a cap: She is supposed to have followed the soldiers towards Philadelphia. Whoever takes up the said servant and secures her in any gaol, so that her master may have her again, shall receive the above Reward and all reasonable charges, paid by John Fourdray. [*Pennsylvania Packet*, July 29, 1776]

[214] Ran away from the Subscriber, a Servant Girl, about 20 Years old, speaks broken English, has had the Small Pox, short thick set, had on a striped Stuff Gown, and redish Poplin Coat; she is a Scotch Girl, and call'd Margaret or Peggy Campbell. Whoever will take up said Girl, and convey her to her Master, shall have Two Dollars Reward, and all necessary Charges paid per Robert Rice. [*Connecticut Journal*, July 31, 1776]

[215] Three Pounds Reward. Run away from the subscriber, living in York town, York county, the 30th day of June, 1776, an Irish servant woman, named Jane Shepherd, about 5 feet 3 inches high, of a fair complexion, pretty fat and lusty, has black hair, and is about 23 years of age; had on, when she went away, a dark brown worsted petticoat, one calicoe bed gown, one calicoe skirt, a cambrick apron, one white halfworn peeling bonnet, and some white linen handkerchiefs; she inclines much to smoking of tobacco, and her under jaw teeth are black. Whoever takes up the said servant, and brings her to her master, or secures her, so that she may

be got again, shall have the above reward, paid by Jacob Doudle. [*Pennsylvania Gazette*, July 31, 1776]

[216] In Mens Clothes. Run away the 30th of July last, from the Jerseys to Philadelphia or New York, a Mulattoe Woman Slave, named Maria; had on a white or red and white jacket, white ticken breeches, white stockings, old mens shoes, and an old beaver hat; she is hardly discernible from a white woman, is rather thinish visage, middle size, thick legs, long black hair, and about 35 years old; she hath left behind her three young children, a good master and mistress, and is going towards New York after a married white man, who is a soldier in the Continental service there. Whoever secures the said Mulattoe in goal, and will immediately advertise the same in this paper, shall have Four Dollars reward. [*Pennsylvania Gazette*, August 7, 1776]

[217] Fifteen Shillings Reward. Ran away from the subscriber, living in Moyamensing township, a mulatto girl named Elizabeth Hector, about 16 years of age, five feet high: Had on when she went away, a linsey petticoat, a black callimanco ditto, a calico short gown, and kenting handkerchief. Whoever takes up said servant and bring her to the subscriber shall have the above Reward, paid by Bartholemew Busiere. [*Pennsylvania Packet*, August 13, 1776]

[218] Run away on the 4th instant, from the subscriber, living in Moreland township, Philadelphia county, a servant Girl named Mary Williams, about 17 years of age, of a low size, but middling thick; had on, and took with her, a long calicoe gown, a short ditto, two other short gowns, one lincey and the other a striped linen one, a blue skirt and two lincey petticoats, four shifts of home made linen, a black bonnet, and a pair of shoes. Whoever takes up said Girl, so that her master may get her again, shall have Six pence reward, and Seven pence for their trouble in bringing her home, paid by Edward Eaton. [*Pennsylvania Gazette*, August 14, 1776]

[219] Run away from the subscriber, 7 miles above Carlisle, an Irish servant Girl, named Catharine Lindon, much pockmarked, a thick chunky girl, with her hair tied, and it is almost black; she is

supposed to be with child; had on, and took with her, one petti-coat, with red, black and white stripes, one fine shift, one bed sheet, one white linen bed gown, one striped ditto, half-worn shoes, and perhaps other clothes that are not yet missed. Whoever secures said girl, so as the owner may get her again, shall have Twenty Shillings reward, and reasonable charges, paid by Robert Darlinton. [*Pennsylvania Gazette*, August 14, 1776]

[220] Three Pounds Reward. Run away from the subscriber, liv-ing in Salisbury township, Lancaster county, an indented servant woman, called Margaret Collins, aged about 30 years, remarkably large, fond of company and drink, and very impertinent and talk-ative when in liquor; had on, and took with her, a red striped lincey short gown and petticoat, a man's beaver hat and shoes, three shirts and two pair of trowsers, one pair checked. Whoever takes up and secures said servant, so that her master may get her again, shall have the above reward, and reasonable charges, paid by John Douglas. [*Pennsylvania Gazette*, September 4, 1776]

[221] Run away, the 19th day of the First Month last, from Josiah Hibberd, of East Whiteland township, in Chester county, an indented servant girl, named Barbara Abercrombie, a Scotch woman, she is bulky and well set, of a fair complexion, dark brown hair, about 27 years of age, speaks in the Scotch dialect; had on, and took with her, a short jacket and petticoat, of brown flannel, one petticoat of blue Bristol stuff, a red and white striped lincey ditto, a check apron, two handkerchiefs, one blue and white, the other red and white, a pair of leather heeled shoes, with sundry other things not remembered; she commonly wears a red and white ribbon on a laced cap, is supposed to be in or near Philadelphia, and was advertised some time since in the Evening Post. As I the subscriber have purchased her time of the above named Josiah Hibberd, do therefore offer a reward of Three Pounds to any person that will secure her in any goal on the con-tinent, and inform me thereof; or Four Pounds, if brought home to my house in Wilmington, in the county of New Castle, on Delaware, with reasonable expences, paid by Caleb Sheward. [*Pennsylvania Gazette*, September 11, 1776]

[222] Fifteen Shillings Reward. Ran away from the subscriber, bricklayer, living in Sixth street, the 23d of July, an indented servant girl named Margaret Cunningham, about seventeen years of age, tall and lusty, something of an Indian look, and has very short thin brown hair. She had on when she went away, a small figured calico short gown, a striped linsey petticoat, no shoes or bonnet, but she has been seen since with a large flowered purple and white short gown, a brown camblet petticoat, and a black bonnet. She served part of her time with George Bakeover, on Germantown road. Whoever takes up said servant, and secures her so that her master gets her gain, shall have the above reward and all reasonable charges. Frederick Walter. [*Pennsylvania Evening Post*, September 14, 1776]

[223] Eight Dollars Reward. Run away from the subscriber, living in Worcester township, Philadelphia county, on Sunday, the 25th of August last, Sarah Craig, an English servant maid; she is about 5 feet high, a dark complexion, has very protuberant eyes, thin and pale visage, speaks very quick, and sometimes pretty mannerly; she had on, when she went away, a long cotton gown, striped with yellow, red, and white; also a half worn black silk bonnet, a large round eared cap, a blue check silk handkerchief, a small striped lincey petticoat, and a large check apron. She stole from her master sundry articles; among them were the following; a new pair of black in the grain pumps, a new, large homespun handkerchief, two short gowns, one of them in white linen, the other calicoe, petticoats, homespun shifts, handkerchiefs, caps, &c. She is very artful and subtil; in order to get a pass the more easily, she told that she had a husband in the camp, at New York, whom she wanted very much to see; but it is well known that her scheme was to go over to the English army, which she is very fond of. Whoever will take up the said servant, and secure her in any goal, and give information thereof to her master, so that he gets her again, or else to Peter Dehaven, in Arch street, between Fourth and Fifth streets, shall have the above reward, and all reasonable charges, paid by Abraham Wentz. [*Pennsylvania Gazette*, September 18, 1776]

[224] Was stolen from the subscriber, in Sadsbury township, Chester county, on the evening of the first of August last, half a

sett of dark calicoe curtains, two calicoe short gowns, one of which had long sleeves, ruffled, one sheet of a ten hundred linen, a lincey check apron, a pair of blue yarn stockings, with red clocks, a pair of high heeled shoes, also a pair of mens shoes, one shirt and a pair of blue and white striped trowsers, a beaver hat, scolloped on the brim; the above goods were stolen by a woman that called herself Peggy Moor, and said she served her time with one Sleator, a Tavern keeper; she had on a black calimancoe petticoat, a white short gown, a black bonnet; wants her teeth before, black hair, a little grey; she could speak Dutch and said she had been living with Dutch people. Whoever secures the above described woman and goods, shall be entitled to a reward of Four Dollars; and any person that can give information of any of the goods, or woman, shall be sufficiently rewarded, by Joseph Park. [*Pennsylvania Gazette*, September 25, 1776]

[225] Six Pence Reward. Absented herself from the subscriber's service, on or about the 25th of September 1775, a certain Juliana Milcahee, about 30 years of age, fresh complexion, black hair and brown eyes, much pitted with the smallpox, is short of stature, broad shouldered and stout made; had on, when she went away, a striped lincey jacket and petticoat, had sundry other clothes with her, that she may change her dress; she had a male child, about 3 months old, which she took with her. Whoever will deliver her to her master, shall have the above reward, paid by Anthony Fortune, at the White Horse and Groom, in Shippen street, near the new Playhouse. [*Pennsylvania Gazette*, September 25, 1776]

[226] Run away from my quarter on Carter's run, some time in May last, a negro wench named Winney; she is about 5 feet 3 or 4 inches high, and of a yellowish complexion. The clothes she commonly wore were a striped Virginia cloth jacket and petticoat, her shift of our own manufactory, and of two thread; but as she took with her a great variety of clothes, I imagine she will frequently change her dress, being an artful subtle wench. She ran away 4 years ago, and got into Maryland, near Port Tobacco, where she passed for a free woman, and hired herself in that neighbourhood several months. Whoever will deliver the said wench to me in Fauquier county, near the courthouse, or to my overseer Thomas

Neavill, on Carter's run, in the said county, shall receive a reward of 5 l. besides what the law allows, and all reasonable charges paid. James Scott, junior. [Purdie's *Virginia Gazette*, September 27, 1776]

[227] Twenty Shillings Reward. Ran Away about a month ago from the subscriber, living in Vine street, an indented servant girl, named Jenny Green, daughter of a certain Nurse Green, of this city, by whom she is supposed to be harboured, or sent down to some of her relations at the Capes; she is about 15 years of age, fair complexion, and pretty lusty: had on, when she went away, a striped short gown, blue stuff skirt, brown bonnet, &c. Whoever takes up and secures the said servant girl, so that her master may have her again, shall have the above reward, and reasonable charges, paid by Francis Harris. [*Pennsylvania Packet*, October 8, 1776]

[228] Run away from the subscriber, the tenth of this instant, an Irish indented servant woman, named Margaret Owings, about 5 feet 5 or 6 inches high; she is a fat, lusty, fresh coloured person, and thought to be with child. She stole, and took with her, sundry wearing apparel, a common linen sheer, marked I.B. a pillow case, and other things not particularly known. Whoever takes up said servant and brings her home, together with what she stole, shall be entitled to Sixpence reward. Joseph Bentley. [*Pennsylvania Gazette*, October 9, 1776]

[229] Ran away on Saturday the 12th instant, from the subscriber, an Irish servant girl named Judith Kennedy, about five feet three inches high, near twenty-seven years of age, is tolerable genteel, pock marked, black hair, and has something of the brogue. She had on, when she went away, a red and white calico short gown, a green skirt, brown cloak, black spotted silk bonnet lined with white, and an old pair of black satin shoes. She also took with her a changeable mantua gown, white dimity petticoat, a fine flowered apron, one check ditto, and two shifts. Whoever takes up said servant and delivers her to me in Water-street, opposite Stamper's wharf, shall receive three Dollars reward, and reasonable charges. John Brown. [*Pennsylvania Evening Post*, October 15, 1776]

[230] Eight Dollars Reward. Run away from the subscriber, in Lower Merion township, Philadelphia county, on the 12th of October instant, a Dutch servant Woman, hath been about two years in the country, speaks very broken English, named Anna Rosina Wenseling, 30 years of age, middle sized, round faced, yellow complexion, thick lips, round shoulders, brown hair, intermixed with white, and bald on the top of her head, a small short thumb on the right hand, large lumps on her big toe joints, much addicted to lying; had on, when she went away, a striped flannel jacket, patched with striped flannel of a darker colour, a petticoat of the same, striped with sheep's black and yellow, and a green worsted under jacket, lined with linen, one tow shift, two tow aprons, a single handkerchief of small check, no shoes nor stockings, an old castor hat. Whoever takes up said servant, and secures her, so as she may be had again, shall have the above reward, and reasonable charges, paid by John Zell. [*Pennsylvania Gazette*, October 16, 1776]

[231] Ran away on Friday, the third inst. a young Negro woman named Bet, of middling stature, thick, fat, and likely, and her ears bored for rings. She had on a black alamode bonnet with lace, an old blue shalloon jacket and petticoat, white linen shift, handkerchief and apron, pale blue worsted stockings with red clocks, high heel black leather shoes and silver buckles. She took with her a half worn scarlet cloak, new purple and yellow checked stuff jacket and petticoat, white linen ditto, blue and white stamped linen ditto, cambrick apron, red and white calico short gown, and black bombazeen quilted petticoat. I have been informed that a Negro woman answering her description, was seen at Brunswick, in Jersey, with some soldiers, but to this I do not give intire credit. Any person delivering the said Negro woman to Mr. Michael Clarke in Chesnut street, Philadelphia, to any of the Maryland officers at camp, or to the subscriber in Charles county, Maryland, shall have Twenty Dollars reward and reasonable charges. Thomas Stone, Philadelphia, October 16. [*Pennsylvania Evening Post*, October 19, 1776]

[232] Eight Dollars Reward. Ran away, on the 10th of October inst. from the subscriber, living in West Nottingham, a Scotch

servant girl, 23 years of age, low and thick set, and has black bushy hair; her left wrist is marked on both sides, having been once broke. She took neither bonnet, cap, stockings or shoes with her, but had on a striped linsey short gown, and walnut coloured petticoat. Whoever takes up said servant, and brings her home, shall have the above reward, paid by James Cummings. [*Pennsylvania Gazette*, October 23, 1776]

[233] Four Dollars Reward. Run away from the subscriber, living in Chester, on the night of the 11th instant, a Dutch servant girl, speaks bad English, about 25 years old, middle stature, fair complexion, and has slits in the under parts of her ears; had on, when she went away, a lincey petticoat, a tow shirt, with sleeves of a finer linen; had neither shoes nor stockings. Whoever takes up the said servant, and brings her to the subscriber, or secures her, so that her master may get her again, shall have the above reward, and reasonable charges, paid by William Kerlin. [*Pennsylvania Gazette*, October 23, 1776]

[234] Eight Dollars Reward. Broke out of the Goal at Lancaster, in the night of the 19th inst. the 3 following prisoners, viz. William Fitzpatrick, about 5 feet 6 inches high, black curled hair, a slim man. Lawrence Cain, about 5 feet 9 inches high, dark coloured hair, a slim fellow. James Parker, about 5 feet 9 inches high, black hair, tied behind, a stout fellow, and belonged to the 7th or 26th regiments of prisoners, now stationed here. Whoever takes up said prisoners, and delivers them at the prison aforesaid, shall have the above reward, or Twenty Shillings for each, and reasonable charges, paid by Peter Riblet, Goaler. At the same time ran away, a servant woman, named Mary Miller, about 5 feet 6 inches high, a stout lusty woman; had on when she went away, a striped cotton petticoat, a calicoe short gown, with red stripes, flowered handkerchief, new cap, new shoes and stockings; talks English and German well. Whoever takes up and secures said servant, so that her master may get her again, shall have Eight Dollars reward, and reasonable charges, paid by Peter Riblet. [*Pennsylvania Gazette*, October 30, 1776]

[235] Four Dollars Reward. Run away from the subscriber, the 21st of October last, an Irish servant girl, named Margaret Kelly, about 5 feet 2 or 3 inches high, she has a scar on the under side of her right arm, black hair, with a high roller; had on, when she went away, a striped calicoe short gown, and a lincey one under it, a striped lincey petticoat, a homespun shift, a tow apron, a white handkerchief, and a white linen bonnet; she walks very upright. Whoever takes up the said servant, so that her master may have her again, shall have the above reward, and all reasonable charges, paid by John Boyer. [*Pennsylvania Gazette*, November 6, 1776]

[236] Run away from the subscriber, living in Kingsess township, Philadelphia county, the 31st of October last, an Irish servant girl, named Jane Gau, of a low size, but pretty fat and thick, of a brown complexion, marked some with the smallpox, has a scar on her under lip, short black hair; had on, when she went away, a new striped homespun linen gown, a purple silk bonnet, almost new, an old black calimancoe quilt, a dirty striped lincey petticoat, low heeled leather shoes, blue yarn stockings; took with her two striped linen short gowns, one a dark stripe, pieced at the sleeves with stripe of another sort, the other a light stripe homespun, almost new, one check apron, one tow ditto, and one purple lincey ditto, two white single handkerchiefs, and one cotton ditto, 3 caps, one lawn the other linen. Whoever takes up the said servant girl, and secures her in any goal, so that her master may get her again, shall have Forty Shillings reward, and reasonable charges, paid by Thomas Laycock. [*Pennsylvania Gazette*, November 6, 1776]

[237] Absented from me the Subscriber, a Negro Slave named Nane, about a Twelvemonth ago, under a Pretence of a Visit, a tall slim Woman; she had on when she went away, a blue Callimanco Gown and other Wearing Apparrel; she is about 27 Years of Age, was formerly a Slave to Mr. Samuel Willis of Bridgwater. Whoever will apprehend or take up said Slave, and convey her to me the Subscriber, or confine her in any of the Goals in this State, shall be handsomely rewarded for their Trouble, and all necessary Charges paid by me, Francis Perkins. [*Continental Journal* (Boston), November 14, 1776]

[238] Three Pounds Reward. Ran Away from the subscriber, living in the Borough of Chester, in the County of Chester, in the night of the 24th of November, a servant girl named Catherine Carr, but sometimes calls herself Pretty Polly, 22 or 23 years of age, about five feet high, hath black hair and a ruddy complexion; had on when she went away, a black silk bonnet, a blue and white calico bed gown with long sleeves, considerably broke, and the body of a long gown under it, a black calimanco skirt, and a green ditto under it, an old shift of fine linen, a pair of thread stockings, and a pair of black grain pumps with odd buckles in them. She stole and carried off the following articles, viz. a pair of white ruffel stays with white lining and a broad stomacher, a brown camblet long gown, and a man's pair of thread stockings. Any person or persons that will apprehend and secure the said servant (it being the second time that she hath absconded) so that her master may have her again, shall be entitled to the above Reward, and reasonable charges if brought home, paid by George Speer. [*Pennsylvania Gazette*, December 18, 1776]

[239] Run away from the Subscriber, on the 17th Instant, a Negro Wench, named Lucy, about 23 Years of Age, this Country born, of a yellow Complexion, and has long Curling Hair: Had on a short striped dark Flannel Gown, a green quilted Petticoat, a blue Baize Cloak, and has other Cloathing with her. Whoever takes up said Wench, and returns her to her Master, shall have Ten Dollars Reward, and all reasonable Charges, paid by Edward Coddington. [*Providence Gazette*, December 21, 1776]

1777

[240] Ran away from the subscriber, living in Market street, Philadelphia, a Scotch Servant Girl named Janet Campbell, of a low stature. She had on, and took with her, a black long gown, printed short ditto, striped linsey petticoat, a new blue oil cloth umbrella, with sundry other articles. It is supposed she is skulking about the barracks. Whoever secures the said servant, in the work-house of this city, shall have One Dollar reward. Robert McNair. [*Pennsylvania Evening Post*, January 11, 1777]

[241] Three Dollars Reward. Run away the 6th of January last, from the subscriber, living in the Northern Liberties of Philadelphia, a Dutch servant woman, named Patty Brannas, about 25 years of age, fresh coloured, black eyes, curled hair, had on and took with her, a black sattin bonnet, a light coloured cloth cloak, with a hood, a calicoe short gown, two striped lincey and one damask petticoats, and a white apron. Whoever takes up and secures said servant, so that her master may have her again, shall have the above reward, and reasonable charges, paid by George Leib. [*Pennsylvania Gazette*, February 5, 1777]

[242] Forty Shillings Reward. Run away from the subscriber, living in Passyunk township, on the 20th of December last, an Irish servant girl, named Patty Pratt, about 16 or 17 years of age; had on, when she went away, a long calicoe gown, green striped petti-coat, two striped linsey ditto, linsey short gown, lawn apron, 3

lawn handkerchiefs, 1 silk ditto, a pair of cotton mittens, half worn shoes, white worsted stockings, white cotton ditto, black bonnet with blue lining. Whoever secures said servant, shall have the above reward, and reasonable charges, paid by Nathan Collens. [*Pennsylvania Gazette*, February 5, 1777]

[243] Twelve Dollars Reward. Ran away on the 27th ult. from the Subscriber, living at Patapsco Neck, about 6 miles from Baltimore-Town, a likely Negro Woman, called Peg, of a middle stature, remarkably slim made, walks quick, is very talkative, and can spell a little, which she is very fond of shewing. It is probable she will endeavour to pass for a free Negro, and it is suspected that some rogue, perhaps a soldier, has carried her off. She had on when she went away, an old shift, half-worn linsey jacket, and black linsey petticoat, with a piece of white before, black stockings, and good shoes. Whoever secures said Negro, so that her master may get her again, shall have, if taken in the county, Eight Dollars, and if out of the county, the above reward, and reasonable charges, if brought home, from Benjamin Eaglestone. [*Maryland Journal*, February 25, 1777]

[244] Stolen, the 20th instant, eight shirts, four cambrick stocks, two pair of stockings, one feather bed and bolster, two blankets, one bed tick, an old sheet, and one pair of shoes. The person who stole the above things, goes by the name of Polly Welsh, otherwise Polly Cambell. She is a well faced woman, brown hair, black eyes, and commonly wears a roul in her hair, has a very comely carriage when in her airs, takes a great deal of snuff, and will get groggy if she can get liquor. She wears a dirty pale green short gown, and sometimes a blue skirt very much worn, a high crown bonnet, and an old white cloak which she borrowed of her neighbour. Any person who apprehends the said Mary, shall have Six Dollars reward by applying to Michael Welsh, Serjeant in the Tenth battalion of Pennsylvania regulars; or to Capt. Lewis Farmer in Second-street, between Vine and Race streets. [*Pennsylvania Evening Post*, February 27, 1777]

[245] Six Dollars Reward. Run away from the subscriber, living in Chester township, Burlington county, a Negroe wench, named

Nancy, about 35 years of age, 5 feet 6 or 7 inches high; had on, and took with her, a chipped hat, with a blue ribbon round it, one red and white short calicoe gown, one striped under ditto, one green quilt, and a striped petticoat. Whoever apprehends the said wench, and confines her in any goal, so that her mistress may get her again, shall receive the above reward, and reasonable charges if brought home. Martha Wallace. [*Pennsylvania Gazette*, March 5, 1777]

[246] Absconded on the 15th instant, from the subscriber, living in Blockley township, Philadelphia county, a servant woman, named Fanny Moore, about 35 years of age, a lusty well set woman, of a swarthy complexion, with black hair, had on a black and white short calicoe gown, blue skirt, and a black silk bonnet; but it is likely she may change her clothes. Whoever takes up and secures said servant in the Work house of Philadelphia, shall have Fifteen Pence reward, paid by Jacob Waggoner. [*Pennsylvania Gazette*, March 26, 1777]

[247] Four Dollars Reward. Ran away from the subscriber, living in Newtown, Bucks County, an Irish servant girl named Ann Henry, 20 years of age, black hair, fresh complexion, much given to drink; had on a striped lincey short gown, yellow petticoat, no handkerchief, apron or bonnet; she was seen going into Philadelphia. Whoever secures said servant so that her master may have her again, shall receive the above Reward from Robert Ramsey. [*Pennsylvania Packet*, April 1, 1777]

[248] Run away last September, from the subscriber, living upon Monk's Neck, about 13 miles above the town of Petersburg, a Virginia born negro wench named Jenny, who carried with her a child named Winney. The wench was very big with child when she went away, is about 25 years old, near 5 feet 2 inches high, and of a yellow complexion. She carried with her a green shalloon gown, a pale blue durants quilt much worn, a white Virginia cloth cotton coat and waistcoat, coat and waistcoat striped with copperas and blue, and another suit checked with blue. The child is between two and three years old, is of a yellower complexion than its mother, and clothed like her. As she generally goes well dressed, I expect she will alter her name and the child's, and

endeavour to pass as a free woman. Any person that will bring the said wench and child to me in Mecklenburg county, near the old courthouse, or give me intelligence so that I get them again, shall have 5 l. reward and be allowed all reasonable charges. Allen Freeman. [Purdie's *Virginia Gazette*, April 11, 1777]

[249] Run away the 15th of March last, from the subscriber, living in Charlestown, Chester county, a Dutch servant Girl, Named Eve Humel, about 15 years of age, something pitted with the smallpox; had on, when she went away, a short lincey gown and petticoat. Whoever takes up said servant, and brings her to her master, shall have Three Shillings and Nine pence reward. Jacob Humen. [*Pennsylvania Packet*, April 16, 1777]

[250] Run away last February, a young Negro Wench named Kate, 14 years old, very lusty, had on when she went away, a new osnaburg gown and petticoat, and a check handkerchief about her head. Whoever will deliver her to me, shall receive Twenty Pounds reward; and I do hereby forewarn all persons from harbouring her upon their peril; she is well known about Stono, and may alter her name. Mary Roybould. [*South Carolina and American General Gazette*, April 17, 1777]

[251] Whereas an indented servant girl named Jane Gray, belonging to Mr. George Gordon of Wilmington, in the Delaware state, did run away on or about the first instant, and made her escape to this city, where she was apprehended and committed to the workhouse, as she refused to return home. The subscriber was desired to send her back, but she took the opportunity to make her escape from him on the 25th instant. She is a slim, ordinary face girl, much pitted with the smallpox, about eighteen or twenty years of age, and dark brown hair. She had on a light ground calico gown, linsey petticoat, cross barred silk handkerchief, and a pair of mens shoes. Whoever apprehends said servant, and secures her so that her master or the subscriber gets her again, shall have Eight Dollars reward, and if brought home reasonable charges paid by George Gordon of Wilmington, or by the subscriber living in Water-street, a little below the Drawbridge. Alexander Graham. [*Pennsylvania Evening Post,* April 29, 1777]

[252] Eight Dollars Reward. Run away from the subscriber, living in Evesham township, in the State of New Jersey, Burlington county, on the 20th of April, 1777, a certain Sarah McGee, Irish descent, born in Philadelphia; she is about 23 years of age, about 5 feet 7 inches high, and very lusty made in proportion; she had on, when she went away, a snuff coloured worsted long gown, a spotted calicoe petticoat, stays and a good white apron, a snuff coloured cloak, faced with snuff coloured shaloon, a black silk bonnet, with a ribbon round the crown: She was seen with her mother, in Philadelphia, who lives in Shippen street, where it is supposed she is concealed. Whoever takes up said servant and brings her to her master, or puts her in confinement, so that her master gets her again, shall have the above reward, and reasonable charges, paid by Barzillai Coat.

N. B. She has a cross on her right arm, put in with gun powder, and the two first letters of her name and the date of the year. [*Pennsylvania Gazette*, April 30, 1777]

[253] Ran away from the subscriber on Thursday last, an English servant girl named Ann Hill, about eighteen or twenty years of age, short, chunky built, likely face, black hair, and wears a roll. She had on, when she went away, a dark purple and white calico long gown, a linsey petticoat with broad stripes, and good shoes and stockings. Whoever takes up said servant shall have Four Dollars reward, and reasonable charges. Peter Sutter. [*Pennsylvania Evening Post*, May 20, 1777]

[254] Eight Dollars Reward. Run away, on the 15th of May instant, from the subscriber, living in Upper Providence township, Chester county, an apprentice girl, about 14 years of age, named Eleanor McIndoe, of a fair complexion, but small of her age: had on, and took with her, two short gowns, one of white linen, the other striped brown and white; two petticoats, one of which is drugget, the back parts striped with red, green, and yellow, the fore parts is striped with blue and brown, 4 and 4; the other is striped with brown and yellow, new shoes, with wooden heels, tied with strings, half worn yarn stockings: It is supposed she is gone with her mother and her elder sister belonging to Daniel O'Neal,

of the city of Philadelphia. Whoever takes up and secures said apprentice in any goal in the province, shall be entitled to the above reward, and reasonable charges, if brought home, paid by John Fox. [*Pennsylvania Gazette*, May 28, 1777]

[255] Ran Away from the subscriber living in Wilmington, a Dutch servant woman named Lena Kime, about thirty years of age, five feet high, thin face, and a scar on her nose; she wears a black bonnet lined with pale red; her other clothes unknown, as she took a good many clothes with her. She is gone with her husband, who is a servant also, and enlisted with Capt. Bartholomew in the Pennsylvania Fifth battalion, commanded by Col. Francis Johnson. It is posed she is gone to Bristol order to get to the camp with the soldiers, therefore it is hoped all those that keep the ferries on Delaware will apprehend said servant, or any other person that secures her in Philadelphia workhouse, shall have Eight Dollars reward and reasonable charges. Moses Bryan. [*Pennsylvania Evening Post*, June 3, 1777]

[256] On Saturday the 7th of June, 1777, was stolen and carried away from the house of the subscriber, in Providence, six yards and one quarter of patch, white ground, with a chocolate stripe; one calico gown, with ruffled cuffs lined with Russian linen; one black double sattin sprigged cloak, with lace round the head and gimp round the cloak; one gauze apron, one spotted handkerchief with a blue stripe round the edge, two pair of cotton stockings, also two thirty dollar bills, and other money; with a number of other articles. The person who stole the said articles calls herself Polly James, alias Polly Young; she is a short thick Irish girl, about 19 years of age; had on when she went away, a black skirt petticoat, a short calico gown with long sleeves, has brown hair, light eyes, fair complexion, and went off without stockings or shoes, and without a bonnet or hat. Whoever will apprehend the said thief, and convey her to Providence, so that she may be brought to justice, shall receive a reward of Ten Dollars, and all necessary charges paid by me, John Dawson. [*Providence Gazette*, June 14, 1777]

[257] Run away from the Subscriber on the 27th of last Month, a Negro Girl named Esther, low of Stature, and well made, about 15

Years of Age, has lost a Joint of a Finger, and formerly the property of Miles King of Hampton; she took with her a white Cotton and red striped Petticoat. I will give a Reward of Twenty Shillings if taken within a Mile of Williamsburg, and Forty Shillings if at a greater Distance. John Shiphard. [Dixon & Hunter's *Virginia Gazette*, July 11, 1777]

[258] Ran away from the subscriber the 14th of June last, a Scotch servant girl named Jennet Stevenson, or may call herself Steinson; she is short and chunky, has a small cast with one eye, light brown hair, fresh colour, and full faced. She had on, when she went away, a striped homespun blue and white short gown, red and blue striped linsey petticoat, the colours dim. She took with her a long calico gown with a pompadour ground, stamped in a lace pattern with small flowers, one white, one check, and two homespun aprons, flax and tow, blue stays with white stomacher, and a plain black mode bonnet with a broad paduasoy riband puffed on it. She was seen with one Thomas Cook going to camp, and was seen coming into town this day with Proctor's artillery, very dirty, in a short gown and petticoat, and barefoot. Whoever secures said servant so that her master gets her again, shall have Eight Dollars reward. Thomas Robbins, Blockmaker, living in Penn-street, near South-street. [*Pennsylvania Evening Post*, July 15, 1777]

[259] Run away from the subscriber in Chesterfield, some time last May, a mulatto girl named Jenny, 5 feet 7 or 8 inches high, her face and neck much run over with ringworms, has a remarkable bushy head of hair, and feet uncommonly large. She had on, and took with her, a narrow purple striped calimanco gown, a petticoat of hair and cotton, a red and white calico do. a white cotton do. and a white waistcoat. I have been informed that she was seen in Southampton, where she passed for a free woman. Whoever brings the said girl to Richmond shall have 10 dollars reward, and reasonable expenses, paid by William Black.

N. B. As I have reason to believe she was enticed from Richmond by some person who lives in the lower parts of the country, and goes by water, I will give 10 dollars to any person who can give me such information as to convict him thereof. [Purdie's *Virginia Gazette*, July 18, 1777]

[260] Run away, on Monday, the 14th instant (July) from John Le Telier, Silversmith, opposite the Coffee house, in Market street, Philadelphia, a Negroe wench, named Nell, about 17 or 18 years of age, short and thick; she carried away with her sundry lincey and linen clothes, a woman's black hat, lined with red, half worn shoes, with large square white metal buckles. Whoever apprehends the said Negroe wench, or secures her in any goal, and gives information to the said Le Telier, or to the subscriber, at the mill, formerly Butler, in New Britain township, Bucks county, shall receive Eight Dollars reward, and if brought home, all reasonable charges. Thomas Hockley. [*Pennsylvania Gazette*, July 30, 1777]

[261] Run away, on the 25th instant, from the subscriber, a servant woman, named Catherine Car, about 21 or 22 years of age, of a black complexion, and middle stature; had on, and took with her, a light chintz gown, one dark ditto, a black silk cloak, black skirt, a good fine shift, striped kenting apron, a white gauze handkerchief, an old brown skirt, old calicoe short gown, and a black silk hat. Whoever takes up and secures said servant in any goal, or bring her to her master, shall have Six Dollars reward, and reasonable charges, paid by Francis McCutchon. [*Pennsylvania Gazette*, July 30, 1777]

[262] Four Dollars Reward. Run away from the subscriber, a Negroe wench, named Hannah, of a middle size; had on, when she went away, a blue serge petticoat, moss coloured jacket, without sleeves, tow shift and apron; took with her a fine shift, a blue quilt, a pair of white stuff stays, a white handkerchief; it is thought she has made towards Philadelphia; she formerly belonged to one Moore, a barber, in Front street; it is thought she has other clothes with her. Whoever secures her in any goal, so that her master may get her again shall have the above reward, paid by Isaac Horner. [*Pennsylvania Gazette*, August 6, 1777]

[263] Was taken in the custody of a certain Catherine Wilson, wife of James Wilson, who was inlisted in Captain Alexander Patterson's company, the following articles, supposed to be stolen from the continental army in the Jersey, viz. a small roan Horse, about four years old, shod before, his hind feet white; a Hessian

cutlass, with a brass handle; a regimental blue coat, turned up with red, a blue vest, without sleeves, and 2 white ditto, 2 white hunting shirts, 8 linen and tow shifts, two pair of ticken breeches, and one leather ditto, 17 pair of stockings, and leggings, old and new, 6 half worn Indian blankets; all the above are supposed to be stolen. Any person or persons proving their property, and paying the charges, may have their goods again, by applying to the subscriber, in Mount Bethel township, Northampton county, Pennsylvania. I am informed that the said woman hath brought from near the camp, on Matutchen in the Jersey, a middle sized bay horse, who is now in this township, supposed also to be stolen; as likewise sundry other goods not specified. Samuel Rea. [*Pennsylvania Gazette*, August 13, 1777]

[264] Run away from the subscriber in Stafford county, the 16th of July, an English servant woman named Margaret Miller (alias Graves) 36 years old, about 5 feet 6 inches high, has black hair and eyes, a number of small black freckles in her face, a remarkable good set of teeth, very large hands and arms, a good skin (though much sun burnt) pitted a little with the smallpox, has a pleasant countenance, is a likely woman, and but spare made. She took with her a cotton shift without wristbands, a jacket and petticoat filled in with black yarn, a striped cotton gown with ruffled cuffs, a black silk bonnet, good linen aprons and caps, two pair of thread and worsted hose, flat heeled shoes, cotton gloves, and a good deal of money. Whoever brings her to me shall have 10 dollars reward. Moses Phillips. [Purdie's *Virginia Gazette*, August 15, 1777]

[265] Three Pounds Reward. Run away, on Saturday, the 17th instant, from the subscriber, living on Mr. Samuel Willer's place, in Moyamensing township, a Dutch indented servant girl, named Barbara Miller; she is about 14 years old, short and fat, has a pretty face, and yellowish brown hair; she had on, when she went away, an old lincey striped petticoat and short gown. Whoever takes up the said servant girl, and brings her back to her master, shall have the above reward, and reasonable charges, paid by Christian Jung. [*Pennsylvania Gazette*, August 27, 1777]

[266] Run away from the subscriber, on the 5th day of June last, an Irish servant woman, named Mary Montgomery, about 5 feet 6 inches high, well set, fresh complexioned, black hair; had on, when she went away, a black and white striped lincey short gown and petticoat, and a black bonnet; she had also a white bed gown, and sundry other clothes with her: It is supposed she went after Captain Matthew Irvine's company, in General Weaden's brigade, now at camp. Whoever secures said servant in Philadelphia goal, shall have Twenty Dollars reward. John Heap. She formerly lived with Major Matthew Smith, of Paxton, in Lancaster county. [*Pennsylvania Gazette*, September 3, 1777]

[267] Was stolen on Saturday night the sixth instant, from the subscriber living in Water street, between Lombard and South streets, near Cuthbert's wharf, an apprentice girl named Jane Baldridge, thirteen years of age, about four feet high, smooth faced, grey eyes, and dark hair. She had on, when she was taken away, a blue and white linsey short gown, an old flannel petticoat very much worn, and coarse brown linen shift with white sleeves. She was stolen by her mother, who says she lives within five miles of Bristol; she is a middle sized woman, fair complexion, large grey eyes, fair hair, and had on a small striped linen gown and petticoat, white stockings, leather shoes, plain black bonnet, and white knit mittens. Whoever informs where the girl can be found, and the mother brought to justice, shall have Eight Dollars reward. Cornelius Hillman. [*Pennsylvania Evening Post*, September 9, 1777]

[268] Run away from the Subscriber last Night, a likely young Negro Wench named Hannah (Daughter of Sykes's Doctor) 18 or 19 Years of Age, a middle Stature, a good Deal like her Father, the well known Fiddler. This is the third Time of her Elopement since the Spring, and I am satisfied she was formerly harboured by ill disposed Persons, who may do so again, unless made aware that I am determined to prosecute them, if detected, and therefore promise a Reward of Ten Pounds on Conviction of the Offender, if a free Person. Hannah was dressed in a fine Virginia Cloth Jacket, bound at the Skirts and Sleeves with Pieces of Calico and Virginia Cloth, Petticoats of striped Cotton and Yarn, white Cotton Shift, Linen

Jane Baldridge, an "apprentice girl . . . thirteen years of age" wears "a blue and white linsey short gown, an old flannel petticoat very much worn." See advertisement 267 from the *Pennsylvania Evening Post*, September 9 1777. Illustration by Eric H. Schnitzer.

Handkerchief, a black Chip Hat, and Shoes and Stockings, she is fond of Dress, and has other Clothes that I cannot describe. Her Hair was lately cut in a very irregular Manner, as a Punishment for Offences, and may now be easily discovered. She is very insinuating, a notorious Thief, and Liar, and will endeavour to pass as a free Person, or frame some plausible Excuse for her Absence. If brought Home to me by any Person (white or black) I will give Eight Dollars Reward. Thomas Fenner. [Dixon & Hunter's *Virginia Gazette*, October 3, 1777]

[269] Seven Dollars Reward. Run away, the 14th inst. a Negro Wench named Bet, born at Flatbush, Long Island: Had on when she went away, a homespun petticoat, and calico short gown. Whoever shall secure the said wench, or give information of any person harbouring her, shall receive the above reward, by me, Philip Lenzi, Confectioner, No. 517, Hanover Square. [*New York Gazette*, October 20, 1777]

[270] Run away the last of September, two negroes. One a wench named Lucy, thirty years of age, five feet three or four inches high, of a yellow complexion, speaks plain, has a scar between her eye brows, and another under her left breast; had on when she went away a black striped Virginia cloth jacket and petticoat. The other a boy named Caleb, twelve or thirteen years old, has a very notable scar on his breast, occasioned by a burn, and has a very sly look; his clothing is of the same kind of cloth as the wench's, and he had on a felt hat. I will give a reward of five dollars for each, if taken in the county; and if out thereof, and confined in any jail, so that I get them again, fifteen dollars each. If brought to me near the courthouse in Caroline county, I will give the above reward, and all reasonable charges. Charles Beazley. [Purdie's *Virginia Gazette*, November 21, 1777]

[271] Ran away last night from the subscriber, living in Water street, near the Crooked Billet, at the sign of the Mason and York Arms, an Irish servant girl named Ann Orr, about eighteen years of age, low of stature, fresh complexion, and dark brown hair: Had on, when she went away, a blue and white striped linen gown, and white linen petticoat and apron. Whoever secures the said servant

in the gaol of this city, or brings her to the subscriber, shall have Twenty Shillings reward, and reasonable charges, paid by Redmond Byrns. [*Pennsylvania Evening Post*, December 9, 1777]

[272] For apprehending and delivering to the subscriber, in Fredericksburg, a mulatto wench named Sally, who ran away about the middle of October last, and went off with a wench belonging to Miss Digges. They have been both in York and Williamsburg. She is of the middle stature, straight and well shaped, has a bushy head of hair, which she generally used to wear dressed up, and has lost some of her fore teeth. She had on a brown worsted damask coat and jacket, but may change her apparel, as she had a variety of clothes. A reward of 20 dollars will also be given for apprehending and delivering to me, a mulatto servant named Hankey (alias Hagai Sexton) who went off about 4 years ago, and has been living these last two years in Albemarle county, where she passed for a free woman, and is still there, protected and harboured by a parcel of free Mulattoes. William Smith. [Dixon & Hunter's *Virginia Gazette*, December 26, 1777]

1778

[273] Ran away on the morning of the thirtieth of Dec. last, from the subscriber, living in Combes's alley, an apprentice girl named Margaret Taggart, of Irish extraction: Had on when she went away, a black silk bonnet with white silk lining, a yellow striped linsey short gown, blue quilted petticoat, yarn stockings, high heeled leather shoes and larges brass buckles; has about four years to serve, and is supposed to be lurking about the barracks. Whoever apprehends her and brings her home, shall receive One Shilling reward and no charges. Jonathan Willis. [*Pennsylvania Evening Post*, January 6, 1778]

[274] Ran Away from her master, living in Kingsess township, Philadelphia county, a servant girl named Ann Powell, of tall stature, down look, and swarthy complexion. Took with her when she went away, a green petticoat, stripe short gown, a brown cloke with a hood, high black bonnet, and sundry other goods &c. It is supposed that she is gone with the army, as she was very fond of soldiers. Whoever takes her up, and brings her to the subscribers shall have Two Shillings and Six-pence reward, and no charges. John Bartram. [*Pennsylvania Evening Post*, January 15, 1778]

[275] Ten Pounds Reward. Ran away, on the evening of the 14th instant, from George Fox's plantation, near Dr. Stevenson's copper mine, in Frederick county, a likely molatto wench, named Sarah; she took with her a molatto boy, about 6 or 7 years old; she also

stole and carried off a man's surtout coat, and a straight bodied ditto, both light colour'd, three mens white shirts, a sum of money, a bed and beding, and many other articles — She went off in the company of Valentine Lind, by trade a taylor, who had been employed in that neighbourhood; 'tis supposed they have one or more horses with them, and may possibly attempt to pass for man and wife.— She is a lusty wench, speaks good English and Dutch, has plenty of good clothes with her, and a large sum of money.— Whoever apprehends said woman and boy, and brings them to the copper mine, or to the subscriber in Baltimore, shall have the above reward, and all reasonable charges, paid by George Somerville. [*Maryland Journal & Baltimore Advertiser*, January 27, 1778]

[276] Run away from the subscriber on Sunday evening the 28th of December last, a negro wench about 19 or 20 years of age, named Clarissa, of the Fulla country, about 5 feet 2 or 3 inches high, stout and well made, remarkably high chested, a small scar on her stomach, one of her upper and one of her lower foreteeth out; had on when she went away, an osnaburgh shift and wrapper of the same, a striped ticking petticoat with calico borders; she took with her a furniture check wrapper red and white, a linen one and sundry other clothes; speaks tolerably good English. A reward of Twenty Pounds will be given to any person or persons that will apprehend and deliver the said wench to the subscriber, or to the Warden of the Work house; and further reward of Fifty Pounds to any person that can convict any white person or persons of harbouring the said wench, and Twenty Pounds if harboured by free or slave negroes, to be paid on conviction by Joseph Gaultier.

N. B. If the said wench will return of her own accord, she shall be forgiven. [*South Carolina and American General Gazette*, March 5, 1778]

[277] Ran away the 24th of February, from the subscriber living in Bilbury, a Scotch servant girl, named Christiana Gunn, about sixteen years of age, about five feet high, fresh complexion, and dark brown hair, long nose, little eyes, broad shoulders, a little pitted with the small pox, thin lips, and wide mouth. Had on when

she went away, a purple silk bonnet, a mixt duffil cloak, a tow shift and old linsey petticoat, a green upper ditto, a mixt coating jacket, a black handkerchief, blue yarn stockings, half worn shoes with low heels, and took with her a tow shift. 'Tis supposed she has gone to Philadelphia to her mother. Whoever secures the said servant in the Burlington gaol, or brings her to me, shall receive two dollars reward and charges, paid by Samuel Robbins. [*New Jersey Gazette*, April 1, 1778]

[278] One Shilling sterling reward. Ran away last night from the subscriber living in Chancery lane, a servant girl named Catherine Cowbelly, about sixteen years of age, of a swarthy complexion and black curled hair; has one year and ten months to serve. Had on and took with her, three long gowns, two calicoes and one camblet; four short gowns, one calico, one striped Holland, one white homespun linen and one linsey; one blue and white petticoat pieced at the bottom of different colours, one new striped linsey ditto, one blue ditto, one blue and white ditto, and one green quilt; four or five handkerchiefs, one new Barcelona ditto, two pair of shoes half worn, pinchbeck buckles, two pair of stockings, two good shifts, three aprons, four good caps, one black paduasoy bonnet and white cloth cloak. Whoever apprehends the said servant and brings her to her mistress, shall have the above reward, and no charges. Eleanor Gislin. [*Pennsylvania Evening Post*, April 6, 1778]

[279] Ran away from the subscriber, living in Third street, a little above Church alley, a Scotch servant girl, named Jane Clark; about 19 years of age, near 4 foot high, chunky made, black hair and a swarthy complexion. She had on and took with her, a striped short crape gown and petticoat, with a long black gown, and other cloathes not yet known. Whoever secures her, so that her master may have her again, shall have Two Shillings and Six-pence reward. John Bates. [*Pennsylvania Ledger*, April 8, 1778]

[280] Ran Away from the subscriber this day, a Negroe wench named Dido, about 26 years of age, a stout well looking hussey; when she went off she wore a striped lincey jacket and petticoat, the rest of her dress unknown. It is supposed some evil disposed persons harbour her in St. Georges or Appoquiniminck Hundreds,

as her acquaintance lay most in those neighbourhoods. Punishment of the most rigorous kind will be administered to those who are found to harbour or conceal the above described slaves. And a reward of Fifty Dollars will be given to any person who will apprehend and secure the said slave in any gaol in the United States, with every reasonable charge, by Humphrey Carson. [*Pennsylvania Packet*, April 22, 1778]

[281] Run away from the subscriber, last Friday, two black wenches, one an old woman about forty years old, named Moll; had on when she went away, a striped waistcoat and blue quilted petticoat. The other a young girl of eighteen, named Diana: Had on when she went away, a striped or dark blue waistcoat, a red cloak with ermine on the fore part of it, and a black hat; the girl is very artful, and may attempt getting on board some of the shipping. Whoever apprehends said wenches, and will deliver them to me, at No. 169, Queen street, shall have Five Dollars reward for each of them. All masters of vessels and others, are hereby forwarned harbouring or carrying them off. Joseph Totten. [*New York Gazette*, May 4, 1778]

[282] Ran away last night, from the subscriber living in Germantown, a lusty, fresh, well-looking servant girl, named Peggy Robeson, about fifteen years of age, pock marked, has a brownish spot about the size of a thumb nail on one of her temples, and her two upper fore teeth do not join. She had on and took with her, a blue shalloon quilted petticoat, three or four homespun linsey petticoats, one of them white, some blue and white striped, and some of a dirty sheep's grey striped, two or three bed gowns of the same, one calico and one white ditto, four or five aprons of homespun flax and tow linen, five or six homespun flax linen shifts, some of them with fine sleeves, neat leather high heeled shoes, and she wears mostly gauze caps. As her sister Sally Robeson was seen with her the day before she went off, it is supposed she has decoyed her away to Elfrith's alley or Chancery lane, where she has been harbouring for some time past; but they will probably go to their father Harry Robeson, who lives about two miles below Chester, near the river. Whoever apprehends said servant girl, and

secures her so that I get her again, shall have Four Dollars reward, and all reasonable charges. Joseph Ferree. [*Pennsylvania Packet*, May 11, 1778]

[283] Run away from the subscriber, a Negro woman, named Hannah, about 19 years old, country born, had on when she went away a striped tow and linen gown an old red shag short cloak, a linen and woolen peticoat, and a striped tow apron. Whoever will take up said Negro and deliver her to the subscriber in the middle parish of Killingly or secure her and send me word shall have 4 dollars reward and all necessary charges paid, by Nath'l Packard. [*Connecticut Courant*, May 12, 1778]

[284] Two Guineas Reward. Run-away on Sunday afternoon last, a negro woman named Venus, about fifty years of age, about five feet three inches high, and inclinable to be lusty: Had on, when she went away, a blue worsted gown, black silk bonnet, and other cloaths not known. As she carried away with her all her cloaths, it is likely she will change her dress. Whoever will bring said wench to her master shall be entitled to a reward of Two Guineas, and all reasonable charges, which will be paid immediately by her master, in Front street, between Market and Arch streets. Walter Goodman. Philadelphia, May 4, 1778.

N. B. As the above wench is well known in this city, it is imagined some of her acquaintance keeps her concealed. [*Royal Pennsylvania Gazette*, May 12, 1778]

[285] Four Dollars Reward. Ran away on the 25th of April, a Mulatto Wench name Patt; had on two striped lincey petticoats, a striped linen short gown, a black bonnet, handsome check handkerchief and a short brown bearskin cloak, half worn shoes and white yarn stockings with blue clocks. Whoever secures said wench in any gaol, so that her master may have her again, shall have the above reward and reasonable charges. George Evans. [*New Jersey Gazette*, May 13, 1778]

[286] Run away from the Subscriber, on Friday the first of May, a young black girl, about 18 years of age named Diona; had on when she went away, a blue and striped waistcoat, blue petticoat, black

hat, short red cloak, with ermine on the fore part; she may attempt getting on board some vessel, whoever apprehends said girl, and will bring her to me, at No. 169, in Queen street, shall be handsomely rewarded. All masters of vessels and others, are hereby forewarned harbouring or carrying her off. Joseph Potter. [*Royal Gazette* (New York), May 16, 1778]

[287] Twenty Shillings Reward. Ran Away from the subscriber, living in Northumberland Town, on Monday night, the 21st of April last, a servant girl named Olive Oatley, about sixteen years of age, five feet high, fair complexion; had on and took with her, a white petticoat, a striped ditto, a short gown of the same, and a white linen bonnet. Whoever secures said servant girl in any gaol of this State, shall have the above reward and reasonable charges, paid by Laughlin McCartney. [*Pennsylvania Packet*, May 20, 1778]

[288] Three Dollars Reward. Run away on Thursday June the 4th, a negro wench named Phillis, she is about 5 feet seven inches high, remarkably stout, about 25 years of age, had on when she went away a black and white striped wooly jacket and petticoat, and a white bonnet. Whoever apprehends said wench and delivers her to Hugh Miller opposite the fly market shall receive the above reward. [*Royal Gazette* (New York), June 6, 1778]

[289] Twelve Dollars Reward. Ran Away last night from the subscriber, living in Manor Township, Lancaster County, near the Blue Rock, a Low Dutch servant girl, about 24 years of age, of a middling size and stature, smooth face; had on when she went away, a yellow petticoat and jacket, and took with her a callico jacket and a white one, white stockings, and shoes tied with strings. It is supposed she went away with a Dutchman, with whom she got acquainted some time ago, of a swarthy complexion and low stature; wears a blanket coat and blue stockings. Whoever secures said servant, so that her master may have her again, shall have the above reward, paid by George Tosh. [*Pennsylvania Packet*, June 10, 1778]

[290] Ran Away on the 21st of January last from the subscriber, a Scotch servant girl named Jenny Cameron, short and thick, of a

dark complexion, has dark brown hair rolled on a string: Had on and took with her a new lincey petticoat and bed gown with brown and white stripes, a lincey petticoat, with red, black and white stripes, one under brown quilt, patched with different colours of linen, an under brown and white petticoat, two new hempen shifts, three lawn caps, four linen handkerchiefs, three white and one purple, two pair of yarn stockings, one blue and the other brown, strong shoes with leather heels, two white tow aprons, and is supposed to have check aprons. Whoever takes up said servant, and secures her in any jail, so that her master may have her again, shall have Ten Dollars reward and reasonable charges, paid by John Speakman. [*Pennsylvania Packet*, July 14, 1778]

[291] Twelve Dollars Reward. Ran away, from the Subscriber's plantation, in Patapsco Neck, on the 10th instant, a young Negro wench, named Peg, about 17 years of age, tall and likely. She had on and took with her, a country linen shift, two linen petticoats, a fine striped linsey ditto, the stripes white, red, yellow and black, and which has been made longer with two or three different sorts of linsey at the top. She was seen at Fell's-Point and Baltimore-Town last Sunday, and it is imagined will attempt to get to camp with the soldiers. Whoever secures said Negro wench, so that her master may get her again, shall be paid the above reward, with reasonable charges, if brought home to John Chapple. [*Maryland Journal*, July 13, 1778]

[292] Ten Pounds Reward. Ran Away from the subscriber, a tall Negro Wench named Sukey Brown; she stutters when she speaks in a hurry; took with her two calico short gowns, one a black and white stripe and other blue and white, a linsey petticoat, and sundry other very good cloaths unknown. It is supposed she is gone off with her husband, James Brown, a free Negro, tall and much pitted with the smallpox. She was born and bred in Bucks County, and formerly lived with one Mr. Vansant. Whoever takes up said Wench and secures her, so that her master may have her again, shall have the above reward and reasonable charges, paid by Philip Moser. [*Pennsylvania Gazette*, July 18, 1778]

[293] Six Dollars Reward. Ran Away from the subscriber, a servant girl named Mary Cann, short and thick, with brown hair and pretty round face, has lost one tooth before, and wears a pretty large round roller, speaks broad English, was born in Devonshire and took shipping in Bristol; 'tis thought she is gone to the Valley Forge to nurse the sick at the Hospital; she commonly wears a short gown and lincey petticoat. Whoever takes up said girl and brings her to the subscriber, or confines her in gaol, shall have the above reward. Mary Nuttle. [*Pennsylvania Packet*, July 30, 1778]

[294] Ten Dollars Reward. Was Stolen from the subscriber, a silk and worsted long gown, a blue quilt, a fine shift, a pillow-case, and fifteen shillings in money; supposed to have been taken by a woman who left Philadelphia when the enemy did, and who has been in the neighborhood every since: she is a short thick woman, pockmarked, with brown hair, and stutters in her speech; had on a black petticoat, a callico short gown, a black bonnet, and was bare footed: Perhaps she may put on some of the stolen cloaths. Whoever takes up said woman and delivers her to Jonathan Gess or Adam Parker, living in Burlington, or Joseph Vandyke in Water-street between Arch and Race-streets, Philadelphia, shall have the above reward and reasonable charges, paid by Israel Wright. [*New Jersey Gazette,* 12 August 1778]

[295] Run away the 4th of August, inst. a negro wench named Clarinda, of a yellow complexion, had on when she went away a cross-bar check coat, a coarse white linen shift, and a blue handkerchief on her head, and formerly belonged to Mrs. Gordon. Whoever will deliver the said wench to the warden of the workhouse in Charlestown, or to the subscribers in King-street, shall receive a reward of fifty pounds currency and all reasonable charges and whoever harbours or entertains her, may depend upon being prosecuted to the utmost rigour of the law. Mordecai & Levy. [*South Carolina Gazette*, August 12, 1778]

[296] Run away from a waggon at Ruffin's ferry about the 1st of July last, a negro wench named Nanny, middle sized, and well shaped. She had on when she left the waggon a blue plains waistcoat and petticoat, and some other clothing with her. She is about

35 years of age, and formerly belonged to Mr. Page of Gloucester, but was lately purchased of Mr. William Finnie of this city. She has a husband at Dixon and Hunter's printing office, and I have been informed has been seen there since her elopement. Whoever apprehends the wench, and delivers her to me in Williamsburg, shall have forty shillings reward. Patrick Robertson. [Purdie's *Virginia Gazette*, August 21, 1778]

[297] Eight Dollars Reward. Ran Away on the 22d of August, from the subscriber in East Marlborough, Chester County, an indented girl named Rachel Scoggin, country born, between seventeen and eighteen years of age, brown skinned, with long black hair, round shouldered, and remarkably proud; had on and took with her, a brown silk bonnet, two caps, a yellowish worsted long gown, a short gown striped with copperas colour, a stamped linen ditto, a striped lincey ditto, a yellowish worsted and linen petticoat, a green striped lincey ditto, one old ditto, two new shifts, one old ditto, one check apron, one fine linen ditto, three tow ditto, one double and two single white linen handkerchiefs, one old silk ditto, one brown ditto, with copperas coloured border, two old linen ditto, a pair of thread stockings and light coloured cloth shoes. It is suspected she has taken several other things, particularly a piece of coarse linen, about ten yards. Whoever takes up and secures said girl so that her master may get her again, shall have the above reward, paid by Moses Pennock. [*Pennsylvania Packet*, September 1, 1778]

[298] Twenty Dollars Reward. Ran Away from the subscriber, living in Whitpain township, Philadelphia county, on the 26th day of September last, a Mulatto Wench named Stiffany, about 16 years of age, middle sized, a smart, active, handy wench; had on and took with her, a black silk bonnet, a calico long gown, four striped linen and lincey short gowns, five lincey petticoats, three shifts, two yards and a half of home made linen, one or two pair of stockings, a pair of shoes, and sundry other wearing apparel. She likewise stole and took with her, a black Horse, five years old, near fifteen hands high, paces and trots, shod before, a star in his forehead, short thick neck, his mane inclining to hand on both sides

of his neck. Whoever apprehends and secures said wench, so that her master may get her and the horse again, shall have the above reward, or Sixteen Dollars for the wench and Four Dollars for the horse, and reasonable charges, paid by David Knox.

N. B. It is very probable she may have a child. [*Pennsylvania Packet*, September 5, 1778]

[299] Ten Pounds reward. Ran away on the night of the eighth instant, a hired servant girl, who goes by the name of Elizabeth Lang. She stole and took with her the following articles, one new fine shift, one white cloth apron, one muslin handkerchief, one black hood handkerchief, one pair of fine sleeves, one fringed muslin cravat, one pair of men's white cotton hose, one painted silk calash, besides sundry other articles not yet known. She is of a darkish complexion, dark hair, about five feet four inches high, chunky made, and country born. Whoever secures said girl with the goods, in any jail of this state, shall be intitled to the above reward, or five pounds for the thief, or goods. James Thomson, at the Black Horse tavern in Market-street.

N. B. Said girl said she left Shamokin for fear of the Indians, &c. [*Pennsylvania Evening Post*, September 11, 1778]

[300] Twenty Dollars Reward. Whereas a woman named Mary came to the subscriber's house in Southwark, on Monday the 7th instant, (September) and agreed with my wife, who has lately brought to bed, to stay with her a week to nurse and attend her; and whilst the family were preparing to go to bed she took the child and went off, and has not since been heard of, although the most diligent search has been made after her: She is about 23 or 24 years of age, round visage, brown hair, was born in England but said she came last from Germantown; had on a long calico gown, red petticoat, and an old fashioned black silk bonnet, but may change her dress as she had a bundle with her: The child is a boy, had on nothing but an old chintz rapper, and is fourteen days old. Whoever takes up the said woman and child, or can give any information where they may be found, shall be intitled to the above reward, and all reasonable charges paid by Daniel Fullan. [*Pennsylvania Packet*, September 12, 1778]

[301] Forty Dollars Reward. Broke Gaol last night, the five following persons, viz. William Brown, an Englishman, thirty six years of age, about five feet seven inches high, fair complexion; had on a blanket surtout coat, sheepskin breeches, yarn stockings and calfskin shoes: He belonged to Capt. Anderson's company at the battle of Germantown, is lame of a wound he received in his foot. Edward Foulke, five feet four inches high, is lame in one of his hands, the fingers very much drawn up: he was committed by John Lea, Esq; for stealing 42 yards of linen from John Augusta, of Christiana hundred. A Negro wench named Jenny Nichols, twenty years of age, and slim; had on a yellow stuff short gown, a blue and white lincey petticoat, and has a Negro child with her about ten months old: was committed as a partner with said Foulke in stealing the linen. Negro Cesar, says he belongs to John page, Kent county; he is very black, has a sour look, about forty-five years of age; had on a white cloth jacket with sleeves, red plush breeches, white yarn stockings, old shoes and one odd buckle; he sometimes wore short petticoat trowsers over his breeches. Jim, a short chunky Negro, about thirty years of age; had on tow shirt and trowsers, a plaid jacket without sleeves; says he lived in Radnor township, and was left free by his mother's will. Whoever takes up and secures said runaways, so that the subscriber may get them again, shall receive the above reward and reasonable charges, at Eight Dollars for either of them, paid by Thomas Clark, Gaoler. [*Pennsylvania Packet*, September 17, 1778]

[302] Twenty Dollars Reward. For securing in any gaol so that the owner may get her again, a certain Negro Wench named Mary, a smart, artful huzzey, about thirty years of age, pock marked, can read tolerable well, pretends to be very religious, and talks somewhat on the Irish accent: Had on and took with her, a brown linen short gown, a black and white striped lincey petticoat, tow shift, half worn wooden heel shoes, a black bonnet, one or two check handkerchiefs, and one blanket. She obtained a pass for three days to look for a master, which time has expired five weeks from this date. She ran away about a year ago and passed for a free woman by the name of Nancy, and it is likely she may do the same now, and change her cloaths. Any person securing her as aforesaid, shall

be entitled to the above reward, paid by the subscriber at Cantwell's Bridge, Newcastle County. John Enos. [*Pennsylvania Packet*, September 29, 1778]

[303] Four Dollars Reward. Ran Away from the subscriber, an apprentice Girl named Mary Eyanson, sixteen years old, a likely girl, with fair hair, about five feet four inches high; she took with her sundry cloaths, viz. a damask gown and blue calimanco skirt, one callico gown, several short gowns, &c. Whoever brings home said Girl shall receive the above reward. Timothy Carrell. [*Pennsylvania Packet*, October 1, 1778]

[304] September 23, 1778. One Hundred Dollars Reward. Ran away, last Sunday morning, the 20th instant, from the subscriber, living in Fairfax County, Virginia, a convict servant man named William OBryan, by trade a weaver; he is about 5 feet 6 or 7 inches high, 30 years of age, of a fair complexion, has a ringworm in his face, and is lame in one of his thumbs, which is shriveled and shorter than the other: Had on when he went away, a blue fustian coat and breeches, home made shirt, thread stockings, country made shoes, a racoon hat, more than half worn; the colour of his jacket is uncertain. It is likely he will change his cloaths, and pass for the husband of a certain Betsey Hanson, as she went off with him. She was born in Pennsylvania, is of thin visage, tall and slender made; had on a linsey worsted gown, wove shoot about, of a yellowish cast, and petticoat wove shoot about with blue and white, black bonnet, and old red stuff shoes. Whoever takes up the aforesaid servant, and delivers him to Mr. David Shields, hatter in Baltimore town, or to the subscriber, living in Fairfax County, Virginia, shall have Fifty Dollars, if taken in Maryland, and if taken in Pennsylvania, the above Reward, paid by Jeremiah Moore. [*Pennsylvania Packet*, October 3, 1778]

[305] Stolen on the night of the tenth inst. a dark calico striped gown, with spots in the stripes, plain made; a purple and white gown plain made; a red sprigged calico gown, a black flowered satin cloke lined with white, also twenty two dollars. The thief is a woman who goes by the name of Mary Brian; she is about twenty four years of age rather lusty, much tanned and freckled, a cast

in her eyes; delights in wearing a coarse black apron; says that she came from New York where she was married to a British soldier, hut sometimes denies her marriage; also says that her mother, Elizabeth Brian, lives in Chester. Whoever secures the goods and thief, shall have Twenty Dollars reward, &c. for the goods only Twelve Dollars. Catherine Todd. [*Pennsylvania Evening Post*, October 7, 1778]

[306] Twenty Pounds Reward for apprehending and bringing home Cuthie, a negro woman who ran away some time in last December, and was formerly advertised by the Reverend John Cameron, of this parish. She is Virginia born, about 28 years of age, near 5 feet 2 or 3 inches high, has a very round face, a remarkable gap between her two lower fore teeth, and a large scar on the outside of one of her legs. Her dress, when she went away, was a coat and jacket of double wove yarn and cotton cloth, striped with blue and yellow, and several articles of tow and cotton cloth, which it is probable she may have changed before now. I have some reason to think that she is gone to York county, where she has several relations at the plantations of Mr. Robert Shield, jun. and Mr. Simon Holiar, at or in the neighbourhood of which places I imagine she is harboured by her connections. Whoever delivers the said slave to me in Mecklenburg, shall have the above reward, or one half thereof if secured in any jail so that I get her again. Robert Munford. [Dixon & Hunter's *Virginia Gazette*, October 16, 1778]

[307] Twenty Dollars Reward. Ran Away, a Scotch servant Girl Named Margaret Morison, about fourteen years of age, short and well set, dark hair; had on and took with her, an olive coloured lincey petticoat, a brown ditto, a striped linen short gown, a light coloured ditto, a white handkerchief, a blue and white ditto, an old white apron, low heel shoes and old thread stockings. Whoever takes up and secures said servant so that her master may have her again, shall have the above reward and all reasonable charges, paid by the subscriber. [*Pennsylvania Packet*, October 17, 1778]

[308] Fifty Dollars Reward. Ran away on the evening of the 7th inst. from Trenton ferry, a likely Mulatto slave, named Sarah, but since calls herself Rachael; She took her son with her, a Mulatto

boy named Bob, about six years old, has a remarkable fair complexion, with flaxen hair: She is a lusty wench, about 34 years of age, big with child; had on a striped linsey petticoat, linen jacket, flat shoes, a large white cloth cloak, and a blanket, but may change her dress, as she has other cloathes with her. She was lately apprehended in the first Maryland regiment, where she pretends to have a husband, with whom she has been the principal part of this campaign, and passed herself as a free woman. Whoever apprehends said woman and boy, and will secure them in any gaol, so that their master may get them again, shall receive the above reward, by applying to Mr. Blair M'Clenachan, of Philadelphia, Capt. Benjamin Brooks, of the third Maryland regiment, at camp, or to Mr. James Sterret, in Baltimore. Mordecai Gist. [*New Jersey Gazette*, October 28, 1778]

[309] Eight Dollars Reward. Ran Away from the subscriber, living in Second street, near the corner of Arch street, Ann Coffin, an indented servant girl, and very talkative: Had on when she went away, which was on Monday morning last, a short linen check gown, green petticoats, and a cloth coloured cloak: It is apprehended she has been decoyed away by some evil disposed person, and that she is harboured in or about the city. Whoever gives information of, or secures the said girl so that her master may get her again, shall have the above reward; and if any person conceals the said girl after this public notice, will be prosecuted by John McFadden. [*Pennsylvania Packet*, November 3, 1778]

[310] Twenty Dollars Reward. Ran Away from the subscriber, on Friday night the second of October last, a likely, lusty, young black wench, named Diana, formerly belonging to Mrs. Ann Griffith; she has large white eyes, and large high breasts: had on when she went away, a black and white short gown, and petticoat of the same; she took with her two tow shifts, a white corded petticoat, and a plain white jacket gathered round the hips. Whoever will bring the said wench home to the subscriber, living at Black Bridge, Apoquiniminck Hundred, Newcastle County, shall be paid the above reward and reasonable charges, by Arnold Naudain, Jun. [*Pennsylvania Packet*, November 24, 1778]

[311] Four Dollars Reward. Run away from the Subscriber, a negro wench, named Bett, born in town, is of a middle size, about 18 years of age, marked with the small-pox; she had on a homespun gown and petticoat. Whoever will secure her and bring her to me shall have the above reward. Misper Lee. [*New York Gazette*, December 21, 1778]

1779

[312] Ran away last Tuesday night, from the subscriber, living in Gray's alley, a Dutch servant girl name Catharine Shutz, about nineteen years of age, broad set, of a good countenance, and speaks broken English. She formerly lived with Anthony Forgenstein, in the Neck, and is supposed to be lurking about the city. Whoever secures her so that the subscriber gets her again, shall have Eight Dollars reward, and reasonable charges. If any person is known to harbour her, he will be prosecuted as the law directs. James Cordill.

N. B. She had on a blue and white striped linen short gown, a new linsey wolsey petticoat, and strong leather shoes. [*Pennsylvania Evening Post*, January 14, 1779]

[313] Run away from the subscriber the 1st of December 1778, a negro wench named Hannah, about 40 years old, has a small beard under her chin, and a scar on one of her arms below her elbow, with a very high sharp nose for a negro, had on when she went away, a country manufactured shift and coat of cotton filled with tow, and a cotton jacket filled with twisted yarn, with a bundle of other clothes. I expect she has made for Paspotank county in Carolina, to one Robert Pendleton's, where she was brought from. Any person delivering her to me, in Dinwiddie county, near Petersburg, shall receive Thirty Dollars reward, besides what the law allows. Henry Vaughan. [Dixon & Nicolson's *Virginia Gazette*, February 12, 1779]

[314] Twenty Dollars Reward. Ran away, last Monday morning, from the subscriber, a young tall Negro Wench, named Peg, about 17 years of age. Had on when she went away, a black and white kersey jacket, a course white linsey petticoat, yarn stockings, and shoes worn down at the heels. She carried with her a young child, a boy, with very bad sore eyes, of whom she had been brought to bed near five weeks; the child had on an old linsey frock, very fine, and she had with her, besides, an old striped linsey petticoat, and an old spotted rug. Likewise ran away, the same day, her husband, who was sent to bring her home; he is a short well-set black fellow, about 5 feet 6 inches high, a big full mouth, down look, named Abraham, has an impediment in his speech when questioned or frightened, is about 25 years of age, and a very artful fellow; he formerly belonged to Alexander Lawson, Esq; and well known about Baltimore-Town Whoever takes up and secures said Negroes, so that their master may get them again, shall be intitled to the above reward, or Ten Dollars for either, with reasonable charges, if brought home, John Chapple. [*Maryland Journal*, March 9, 1779]

[315] Forty Dollars Reward. Ran away last night, a Negro Wench named Hannah, about thirty years of age, a short, thick, active woman; she took with her a linsey woolsey jacket, a blue and white calico gown. Her husband, a free Negro Man called Will, went off with her; he is middle sized, about thirty-five years old, has the appearance of a soft, silly fellow, and is given to liquor. The above reward will be given for apprehending the Wench, and all reasonable charges paid by John Ewing. [*Pennsylvania Packet*, March 20, 1779]

[316] Sixty Dollars Reward. Ran away last night from the subscriber, a servant woman named Mary O'Brian, but sometimes calls herself Mary De, which was her last husband's name, and formerly lived at Chrisman's Mill, near the Valley Forge: She is about thirty years of age, middle size, fair hair, grey eyes, stoops in her walk, and has the broague on her tongue. She stole and carried off with her, one black cloth cloak, one white silk bonnet, one long callico gown, two white linen short gowns, one striped ditto, two striped lincey ditto, one brown skirt, one white diaper ditto, one

white linen apron, two coarse ditto, two coarse shifts and one fine ditto, one new cross-barred silk handkerchief, one lawn ditto, one cambrick ditto, one pair of white cotton mitts, one cap with a broad border, one pair of blue stuff shoes, one pair of calf-skin ditto, one pair of mens shoes, one pair of thread stockings, and many other articles too tedious to mention. Whoever secures the above articles so that the owner may have them again, and delivers the servant to her master in Chester, shall have the above reward and reasonable charges, paid by Joshua Vaughan. [*Pennsylvania Packet*, May 4, 1779]

[317] Went off from the Subscriber, of this town, the 18th inst. a Negro Wench, called Peggy, about 26 years of age, talks on the Welch accent, her complexion of a yellowish cast. Had on, and took with her, two short gowns (or bed-gowns) one of white linen, the other calicoe, one side purple and white, the other black and white, much faded, a blue petticoat of duffil cloth, two osnabrug shifts, good shoes, &c. Forty Dollars will be paid the person who secures her in any gaol, so that I may get her again. Robert M'Crea, of Alexandria. [*Maryland Journal,* May 4, 1779]

[318] Run away from the subscriber on Wednesday the 8th of April last, a stout negro wench named Cloe, about 24 years of age, formerly the property of Capt. Muncreef, speaks pretty good English, and is of a yellowish complexion; had on when she went away a blue and a white petticoat and the body of a mans light blue sagathy coat; she was pursued and seen last Friday with a mulatto fellow named Nero, the property of Mr. Mucklewrath, who is also runaway. It is supposed the wench continues with him, and is come towards Charlestown. Whoever will apprehend the said wench or fellow, and deliver either of them to the Warden of the Work-house, shall receive One Hundred Pounds currency each, and all reasonable charges from the said Warden, or the subscriber at Walnut branch, Four holes. Martin Pfeniger. [*South Carolina and American General Gazette*, May 29, 1779]

[319] Three Hundred Dollars Reward. Last night ran away from the subscriber, a Negro man and Negro girl, the man about 25 years old, thick, well built, speaks low, and shews his teeth when

he speaks, has a down look, this country born, his name is Bud, the girls name is Nabey a short thick sett full faced girl, about 20 years old, low spoken, a subtle crafty creature; it is most likely their design is to get on board some privateer, and its probable the girl may be dress'd in mens cloaths; the man is about 5 feet 8 inches high, both well cloathed. Whoever shall take them up and return them to me, or give such notice of their being secured, as I can obtain them, shall have the above reward of three hundred dollars, two hundred for the man only, or one hundred for the girl only, and reasonable charges paid, by Edward Hinman. Fifty dollars reward will be given to any one who will return to the subscriber in Woodbury a Negro girl named Lettice, about 24 years of age, trim built and speaks good English, who it is supposed went away with the above Negroes. [*Connecticut Courant*, June 8, 1779]

[320] One Hundred Dollars Reward. Ran away from the Subscriber, on the 28th instant, a tall likely Negro Wench, named Nanny, about 25 years of age. Had on, and took with her, 1 Indian calico gown, 1 new black and white linsey petticoat, one old striped ditto, 1 white linen handkerchief, 1 single ditto, 1 pair of high-heeled shoes, and a felt hat. Whoever secures the said Wench, so that I may get her again, shall have, if taken up within the County, Fifty Dollars; and if out of the County, the above Reward, and reasonable charges, if brought home. Michael Kewan. [*Maryland Journal*, July 20, 1779]

[321] Run away from the subscriber on Thursday the 1st of this instant (July) two negroes viz. Persilla and Joan. Persilla supposed to be about 18 years old, had on when she went away such clothes as house negroes usually wear, but carried sundry others with her, particularly a blue calimanco quilt, lined with green shalloon, has her ears board for bobs, and carried several pair with her, I bought her some time last summer of Major Cowper, at Suffolk, and formerly the property of Captain Wright, at Crany island. Joan about 16 years old, had on when she went away, a new osnabrugs shift remarkably touched with iron mould, a mixed black yarn petticoat, and jackcoat of white do. one half the sleeve of which the same as the coat, a blue tammy quilt patched before with blue shalloon. I bought her of Mr. William Relly of Lancaster county,

and have reason to believe they were carried off by water. Imagine they will make for Nansemond or Princess Anne county. Whoever will secure them so that I may get them again, shall receive 50 l. reward, or if delivered to me in Petersburg 100 l. All masters and owners of vessels are hereby forwarned from carrying them off at their peril. William Colvin. [Dixon & Nicolson's *Virginia Gazette*, July 31, 1779]

[322] Twenty Dollars Reward. Run away from the subscriber, living in Upper Dublin township, Philadelphia county, on the 13th day of July, a Dutch Servant Maid, named Carolina Bosinger, alias Lania, about 30 years of age, she has lost one of her eyes, and has a thin spare visage, with black hair, a middle sized woman, and talks bad English; had on and took with her 5 short gowns, 2 calico, 1 linen, 1 worsted stripe, 1 linen stripe, 3 linsey petticoats, 2 white aprons. She was imported some years ago, and purchased by Peter Miller, living in Northampton, and sold to John Hist, sold again to George Snider, and sold again to John Garat, and purchased by the subscriber. Whoever takes up and secures the said servant, so that her master may have her again, shall receive the above reward, and reasonable charges, paid by Arthur Broades. [*Pennsylvania Gazette*, August 4, 1779]

[323] One Hundred Dollars Reward. Was stolen last night from the subscriber living at the Unicorn tavern, on Lancaster road, 16 miles from Philadelphia, the following articles, viz. between nine and ten yards of half whitened linen of 1100, five cuts of brown thread, two fine shifts, one fine apron, one check ditto, two striped linen short gowns, one striped cotton skirt, three yards of striped cotton the same as the skirt, one black silk bonnet with a drawed crown, a light coloured cloth cloak, one pair of men's shoes, a silver stock buckle, and several other articles. The above articles were stole by a woman, who goes by the name of Katey Black, a short chunky body, of a dark complexion, black hair; had on a striped linen short gown, two lincey petticoats, one of a very broad stripe, which were all the clothes she had before she stole the above. Whoever takes up and secures said thief with the above articles, or any of them, shall have the above reward, and reasonable charges, paid by Robert Canady. [*Pennsylvania Gazette*, August 6, 1779]

[324] One Hundred Dollars Reward. Ran away from Hager's town, Washington County, Maryland in September last, a Negro wench named Peggy, but sometimes calls herself Nancy, about 26 years of age, talks on the Welsh accent, her complexion of a yellowish cast, the wool on her head is longer than negroes commonly have: Had on a blue petticoat of Duffil cloth, old shoes and stockings, her other clothes uncertain. It is supposed she went off with a Portugese fellow who served his time with Mr. Jacob Funk: they probably may be in the neighborhood of Georgetown or Alexandria or gone towards camp, and that she will attempt to pass for a free woman, and wife to the Portugese fellow. Whoever takes her up and secures her in any gaol, so that the subscriber get her again, or delivers her to Daniel Hughes, Esq., in Hager's town, shall have the above reward, and reasonable charges, John Swan. [*Maryland Journal*, October 11, 1779]

[325] Thirty Dollars Reward. Ran away from the subscriber, living in Somerset county, Bedminster township, on the 25th of October last, an apprentice girl, named Massey Doyl, between 14 and 15 years of age, brownish hair, sandy complection, and something of a down look; had on and took away with her, one long gown of striped purple callico, check apron, old red cloak, a pair of stays, three lincey petticoats, one blue, the other two of a reddish brown collour; three striped short gowns, one of linsey, the other two of tow and linen; a black silk bonnet, a round ear'd cap and ribbon, old blue yarn stockings, old pumps with steel buckles, some blue stocking yarn, a pair of pillow cases marked L R, and several other things. Whoever will secure the said girl, or give intelligence so that the owner may get her again, shall have the above reward, and all reasonable charges, paid by John Barkley. [*New-Jersey Journal*, December 14, 1779]

1780

[326] One Hundred Dollars Reward. Ran away on Monday morning the 20th instant, an Irish servant girl named Jane Smith, about five feet six inches high, black hair, a down look, remarkably freckled in her face; had on and took with her, a striped short gown, striped lincey petticoat, a pair of new stockings, new shoes, and a new check handkerchief: She stole and took with her a dark grey cloak almost new, a green bonnet with a white ribbond round it, a pair of silver shoe buckles, a pair of white mitts, and about forty dollars in Continental money. Whoever takes up the said servant and secures her in any gaol in this State, so that her master may have her again, shall have the above reward, and reasonable charges if brought home, paid by Jacob Keehmle.

N. B. The above Jane Smith is a noted thief, and was concerned in a great robbery in July last. [*Pennsylvania Packet*, January 1, 1780]

[327] Absented from her Husband, Hannah, the wife of Joshua Burn, and has taken along with her a roccolo coat and three good Holland shirts, almost new, one pair of silver buckles, two pair of new yarn stockings, and sundry household goods, too tedious to mention. These are therefore to forewarn all persons not to trust her on my account, for I will not pay any debt of her contracting after this date. Joshua Burn. [*Pennsylvania Gazette*, January 19, 1780]

[328] Run away from the Subscriber, living in South Kingstown, an Indian Servant Woman, named Patience, about 30 Years of Age, short and thick, has a Scar on one Side of her Face, and is very talkative. Had on, when she went away, a black quilted Petticoat, somewhat worn, a spotted green woollen Cooler; a blue Cloth Bonnet; and took with her a large white Blanket. Said Indian has been known to change her Name. Whoever will take up said Servant, and secure her in any of the Gaols of the United States, so that her Master may have her again, or return her to her Master in South Kingstown, shall have One Hundred Dollars Reward, and all necessary Charges, paid by Stephen Potter. [*Providence Gazette*, February 26, 1780]

[329] Run away yesterday morning, a Mulatto Girl, 14 or 15 years old, slim made, long hands and feet; had on a flowered red and green flannel petticoat and blue cloth jacket. Any person that brings her to No. 870, Dock street, shall be handsomely rewarded. [*Royal Gazette* (New York), May 3, 1780]

[330] Ran away this morning from the subscriber, a Negro Wench, named Maria, alias Amoritta; she is about 34 years of age, tall and well made, her face long, and features more regular than are common with her colour; she had on, or took with her, a pale blue and white short linsey gown and petticoat almost new, a petticoat of green baize, a pair of new high-heel'd leather shoes, good shifts of brown homespun linen, and aprons of the same. It is supposed she will endeavour to get into the Jersies, as she came from thence, and once lived with Mr. Thomas Lowrey, of Flemington, but it is suspected she is now lurking in this city, or concealed by some free negroes. She also took her female child with her, named Jane, about 4 years old, well made, fat, round faced, and lively; had on or took with her, a brown homespun frock, also a blue and white linsey frock. Whoever will deliver the said wench and child to the subscriber in Philadelphia, shall have the above reward. John Duffield. [*New Jersey Gazette*, July 19, 1780]

[331] Run away from the subscriber last Sunday night, a young mulatto wench named Sukey. Her dress when she went away was white Virginia cloth, a linen bonnet made in the fashion; she has a

large bushy head of hair, her upper fore teeth much decayed, and some of them out, which causes her to lisp, shows her teeth when laughing, and is very brazen and impertinent. She can wash, iron, and cook. I expect she will make to some town or public place, and may attempt to pass for a free wench. Whoever delivers the said wench to me in Newcastle, shall receive a reward of one hundred pounds if taken fifty miles from this place, and in proportion for a greater or lesser distance. William Tinsley. [Clarkson & Davis's *Virginia Gazette*, August 19, 1780]

[332] Eight Dollars Reward. Run away on Sunday night last, a Negro Girl named Jenny, about 14 years of age, a native of Georgia, from whence she came in the last fleet with her owners; she is of a very black complexion, much marked with the small pox which she had not long since, has remarkable red eyes, short curl'd eye lashes and has lost one of her fore teeth of her underjaw: She had on when she went away a black callimanco coat, a white linen wrapper and cap, and carried off all her other clothes with her. The above reward will be given to any person on delivering her to Mr. Dole, No. 128, Great Dock street, or give such information so as she may be taken; She was seen yesterday with some sailors on one of the docks. Captains of vessels and others are cautioned against harbouring her. She is a remarkable thief and liar. [*Royal Gazette* (New York), September 6, 1780]

[333] Run away from the Subscriber on the 16th day of September instant, a Negro Wench named Rose, she is about the middle size, is a handsome black, and has an impediment in her speech; had on when she went away a green stuff petticoat, a red and white calico short gown, a red silk handkerchief, and a black sattin bonnet. Whoever brings her to me the subscriber, or secures her, shall, upon application, at No. 55, Queen street, receive Five Dollars Reward, and all charges. Alexander Zuntz. [*Royal Gazette* (New York), September 20, 1780]

[334] Committed to the jail of Charlotte county, Dinah, a negro wench, who says she belongs to John Adderson of Northumberland, she appears to be about 40 years of age, has a blemish in her right eye, has on a white country cloth waistcoat; a

rolls petticoat and shirt, much worn. The owner is desired to take her away and pay charges. Robert Rakestraw, Jailer. [Dixon & Nicolson's *Virginia Gazette*, October 18, 1780]

[335] Run away from the subscriber near Petersburg, on Thursday the 2d instant (November) two negro slaves, viz. Marcus, a small well set fellow, about 5 feet 4 or 5 inches high, and African born, speaks very broken English, and is about 40 years of age. Nanny, who formerly belonged to the estate of Edward Cocke of Charles City. She run away about two years ago, and was harboured some time in that county, and afterwards was taken up in Hampton where the passed some times as a free woman by the name of Nanny Lymus, has a husband by the name of Charles (a fiddler) belonging to Mr. Masterson in New Kent. She is a likely sensible wench, of a yellowish complexion, about 5 feet 7 or 8 inches high, has bad teeth, and about 35 years of age (Virginia born) had on when she went away, a white yarn petticoat wove serge, and jacket of mixed black and white Virginia cloth. She took with her a number of other clothes, and it is possible may change her dress. The fellow was clothed as in usual for labouring negroes, though very probable will change his dress. Whoever will deliver the said slaves to the subscriber, or secure them in any jail so that I get them again, shall receive 1000 dollars reward, or 500 for either. Richard Taylor. [Dixon & Nicolson's *Virginia Gazette*, November 18, 1780]

[336] Run-Away from the subscriber on Thursday the 14th instant, a tall Negro Wench, named Phillis, had on when she went away a white negro cloth jacket, with blue sleeves, a calico coat, an old red cloak, and a pair of large black ear bobs in her ears; she has a remarkable scar on her nose, and as she is well known in town, it is very probable she will hire to wash and cook. One Guinea reward will be paid on delivery of said wench to the subscriber. All persons are forbid harbouring her, as they will answer the same at their peril. Dorcas Holmes. [*Royal South Carolina Gazette*, December 21, 1780]

1781

[337] Ran away from the subscriber the beginning of this month, Two Negroes, viz. York, who had on when he absconded an old blue coat of the Hessian uniform, wants several of his fore teeth; also Priscilla, his wife, a likely young wench, born in this country, had on when she went away a blue Bath coating wrapper and petticoat; they were formerly the property of Jonathan Bryan, Esq. Whoever will deliver the above Negroes to John Morel at Bewlie, or to the subscriber in Savannah, shall receive one guinea reward for each of them; and ten guineas will be paid to any one informing of their being harboured by a white person, or conviction on a black person. Peter Henry Morel. [*Royal Georgia Gazette*, January 18, 1781]

[338] Ran away, from the subscribers last night, a negro man named Joe, and a negro woman named Hester: The man is about five feet six or seven inches high, well set, full faced, of an open countenance, was formerly a servant to a British officer, speaks the German language well; had on and took with him a brown great coat badly dyed, white pewter buttons with the letters U. S. A. in a cypher, a green coat with red cuffs and cape and yellow buttons, white jacket and leather breeches, a pair of boots and a pair of shoes, two or three pair of stockings, and two or three shirts. The wench is small though well made, and has a lively eye, being bred in Carolina has the manners of the West-India slaves; she had on a red striped linsey short gown and petticoat, and took with her a

dark brown cloak and sundry other clothes. Whoever takes up and secures the above Negroes shall receive Six Spanish milled dollars each, and reasonable charges. Robert L. Hooper, Robert Hoops. [*New Jersey Gazette*, January 24, 1781]

[339] Ran away from the subscriber on the 29th ult. a mulatto girl named Agnes Beat had on when she went away, a dark linsey gown and petticoat, light colored cloak, black bonnet, low heel'd shoes and as she has taken with her sundry other clothes, she may alter her dress. Whoever takes up said Mullatto shall have three hundred dollars reward and reasonable charges paid by me Adam Van Hart. [*New Jersey Gazette*, February 7, 1781]

[340] My Negro Wench named Pleasant Queen Anne, ran away on the 18th instant, and had on a red moreen petticoat, a brown short gown, with white lining, a pair of brown rib'd stockings. Whoever will bring her to me shall receive Forty Shillings reward. John Curry, No. 30, William Street. [*Royal Gazette* (New York), March 3, 1781]

[341] Ran away from the subscriber in January last, a Negro Girl, named Nan, about 12 years old, had on a blue wrapper and petticoat, speaks good English, is branded MR on her face and right breast. Whoever brings her to No. 64, near the church, shall receive three dollars reward. It is requested that no person do harbour her on any pretence; any offending in this respect will be prosecuted as the law directs. Wm. Cross. [*Royal Georgia Gazette*, March 8, 1781]

[342] Ran away from the subscriber, last night, a Scotch Servant Girl, named Christiana Gun, about 19 years of age, about 5 feet high, well set, a little pitted with the small-pox, has a large nose, talks good English: had on and took away with her, 2 linsey petticoats, the one a red the other a blue stripe, a blue ground chintz short gown, one ditto, linsey, one ditto, red stripe linen, home made, &c. &c. Whoever takes up and brings the said Girl to me, in Front street, near Race street, shall be handsomely rewarded. Jacob Hart.

N. B. All persons are forbid to harbour said Girl at their peril. She is an arch Thief. March 19. [*Pennsylvania Packet*, March 27, 1781]

[343] Ran Away in July last, a Negroe Woman, named Sue, about 45 years of age; has a down look, remarkable large breasts, and a wen upon the temple; but as she is very artful, she may endeavour to hide it by a long ear'd cap she generally wears; she discovers the loss of some of her teeth when she laughs: She had a variety of clothes, among which are, a tartan, a white linen, and a calico gown, and a striped silk jacket. She passed in Baltimore, where she remained for some time, by the name of Free Poll. She is now about Philadelphia, waiting for the return of her husband, as she calls him; a free Mulattoe, named Mark Stubbs, who sailed from Baltimore in a ship called the Enterprize: He is a short thick talkative fellow, about 50 years of age, and a most notorious villain. She is a good cook, can wash and iron well; he is a butcher, and it is probable they may set up for themselves about the city. Any person who will secure her in any goal in the United States, shall have a Reward of Five Pounds Specie, or if delivered to Mr. James Heron, in Philadelphia, or to the subscriber, at Greenburry's Point, near Annapolis, Ten Pounds Specie. David Kerr. [*Pennsylvania Gazette*, May 16, 1781]

[344] Three Pounds in Gold or Silver Reward. Ran away on Sunday night last, the 27th of this instant, from the subscriber living in Newtown Buck's County Pennsylvania, a negro woman named Fann, a short thick wench, about 18 or 19 years of age, very black, thick lips; had on a short gown and petticoat made of linsey black and white stripes, a large bundle of other cloths for herself and female child about three years old; it is expected she has been assisted by some negro or mulatto. Whoever takes up and secures said Negro wench and child, so that her master may have them again, shall receive the above reward paid by Samuel Yardley. [*New Jersey Gazette*, June 6, 1781]

[345] Ran away, on the 3d of June, a Servant Girl, named Rachel Fitzpatrick, about seventeen years of age, she is a short fat girl, of a ruddy complexion; had on a white gown and linsey petticoat, and

took with her sundry other cloaths. John Vanderen. [*Freeman's Journal* (Philadelphia), June 20, 1781]

[346] Run away, a likely Mulatto Wench, called Pamelia, 18 years old, about five feet three inches high, stout and well made, had on when she went away, a short purple callicoe gown and pink petticoat. Whoever apprehends and will conduct her to the subscriber in Dutch street shall be grately rewarded. All persons are cautioned from harbouring or carrying her off the Island. Elizabeth Evans. [*Royal Gazette* (New York), June 27, 1781]

[347] Ten Hard Dollars Reward. Run Away this morning from the subscriber, A certain Negroe Woman, called Bett, of middle stature, about 21 years of age: Had on a straw hat, covered with green silk, a long red striped calicoe gown, a brown linsey petticoat, a striped lawn apron; as she took with her a black calimancoe petticoat and many other articles, it is probable she will change her dress; she also took with her a female child, of about three years of age: It is supposed she is either in Philadelphia or gone towards Virginia in company with two white men. Whoever takes her up, and secures her in any goal, that her master may have her again, shall have the above reward, and all reasonable charges, if brought home, paid by Jacob Phillips. [*Pennsylvania Gazette*, July 18, 1781]

[348] Five Dollars Reward. Run away from the Subscriber, on Tuesday the 3d instant, a Negro Wench named Luce, about twenty-eight years old, has a large mark on one of her cheeks which looks like a scar, she had on when she went off, a homespun short gown and petticoat. Whoever takes up the said wench and secures her, or gives information so that her mistress may get her again, shall receive the above reward, from Ann Price, on Golden Hill, next door to the corner of Fair street.

N. B. If the aforsaid wench will return, she will be forgiven. [*Royal Gazette* (New York), July 21, 1781]

[349] Run Away on Monday night, nine o'clock, from John O'Brien, at the Four Alls, near the Ferry Stairs, a young negro girl named Sarah, about 19 years old, she wore a white short gown and

a cotton petticoat. Whoever returns her to her master, or gives information for her recovery, shall receive eight Dollars reward. All masters of vessels and others are forewarned against harbouring her at their peril. [*Royal Gazette* (New York), July 25, 1781]

[350] Ten Hard Dollars Reward. Ran away last night, from the subscriber, a Negro Man named Frank, about 40 years of age, 5 feet 8 or 10 inches high, slender made, has small legs, remarkable large flat feet, stoops and hobbles very much in his walking; had on or took with him a long brown broad cloth coat, a pair of blue plush breeches, several cloth jackets, some tow shirts and trowsers. Also ran away at the same time, a Negro Wench named Phoebe (wife of said Negro man) about 40 years of age, very talkative, active, and smart; had on or took with her a dark brown chintz gown, a black calimanco quilt, some short gowns and petticoats, besides several things she has stolen. She also took with her her male child named Obadiah, about 18 months old, but small for his age; he has a very large head and crooked legs. Whoever secures the said Negroes, that the subscriber may have them again, shall receive the above reward, and reasonable charges if brought home, paid by John Wilson. [*New Jersey Journal*, August 8, 1781]

[351] Five Dollars Reward. Run away on Monday afternoon, from the Subscriber, living at No. 14, Golden Hill Street, a mulatto Wench named Jane, about nineteen years of age, four feet, six or seven inches high, middling likely, had on or took with her two light coloured callico short gowns, a black callimanco skirt and old stuff shoes. Whoever secures the said wench so that her master may get her again, shall have the above reward paid by Joseph Thomas. [*Royal Gazette* (New York), August 15, 1781]

[352] On the Night of the 24th Instant the House of the Subscriber, in Cranston, was broken open, and the following Articles were stolen, viz. One Chintz Gown, one Worsted Ditto, one Holland Apron, one Holland Shift, one Tow and Linen Ditto, one Holland Shirt, one Holland Sheet, one Tow and Linen Ditto, one striped Linen Petticoat, two Silk Handkerchiefs, two Lawn Ditto, one Pair of Thread Stockings, Half a Yard of new Cambrick, on Yard of Gold Lace, and several other Articles. The Person who

committed this Robbery is supposed to be an Indian Woman, that has been in the Neighbourhood sometime, and called herself Sarah Phillips, therefore, whoever will take and secure the said Indian Woman, so that she may be brought to Justice, and the Goods recovered, shall receive Ten Silver Dollars Reward. Gideon Westcott. [*American Journal* (Rhode Island), August 29, 1781]

[353] Run away from the Subscriber Oct. 1, 1781, a Mulatto Girl named Diana, about 14 years of age, about four feet high, stout and well made, rough face, and had on when she went away a short red callico bed gown, osnaburgh petticoat, and a blue check hand-kerchief, she was bought of Mr. Newton the 4th of June 1781. Whoever apprehends or gives information on to the Printer, so that the said run away may be had again, shall receive Five Dollars reward. Any person or persons harbouring or concealing the said runaway, shall be prosecuted as the law directs. [*Royal Gazette* (New York), October 10, 1781]

[354] Run away from the subscriber on Thursday last a Negro Wench, named Peg, about 18 years of age, born in Carolina, had on when she went away a blue cloth jacket with long sleeves, made in the form of a riding dress, with bright yellow buttons; this is to forwarn all persons from harbouring her and all masters of vessels from carrying her out of this port upon the penalty of paying whatever the law directs. Whosoever will take up the said Negro, and bring her to No. 48, Cherry Street, shall receive One Guinea reward. William Willson. [*Royal Gazette* (New York), November 17, 1781]

1782

[355] Run away from the subscriber, on the 3d of January, a fat lusty Negro Wench, named Rachel, had on when she went away a dark callicoe short gown and homespun petticoat, without cloak or hat. Whoever will secure said wench so that the owner may recover his property shall receive Four Dollars reward from me David Blair, No. 30, Little Dock Street. [*Royal Gazette* (New York), January 9, 1782]

[356] Three Pounds Reward. Ran away from the subscriber, living in Long-Green, Baltimore County, about the middle of December last, a likely well-made Negro Wench, about thirty years of age, five feet two or three inches high; had on and took with her, an old red outside petticoat, an under linsey ditto, an old calico jacket, a linsey inside ditto, a white silk bonnet, faced with red, flat-heel'd shoes, and blue yarn stockings. Whoever takes up the aforesaid described Wench, and secures her, so as I may have her again, shall receive Thirty Shillings reward, and the above reward if brought home, and reasonable charges, paid by me. Francis Coskery.

N. B. She was bought by the subscriber from Mr. John Casey, of Baltimore-Town and Mr. Casey purchased her from Mr. John Burges, in Upper-Marlborough, in Ann-Arundel County, where I think she is gone. [*Maryland Journal*, February 5, 1782]

[357] Run away from her Master on Monday morning last, a Negro Wench, named Jane, she had on a pale green callimanco

petticoat, a red short gown, a scarlet cloak with a hood on it; about fifteen years of age, very talkative and speaks very good English. Whoever takes up said Negro Wench, and brings her to Francis Doyl, No. 63, Chatham Street, shall have Two Dollars reward. [*Royal Gazette* (New York), February 7, 1782]

[358] Two Guineas Reward. Run away, on the 28th instant, a Negro Wench named Lissa, the property of John Carow, had on when she went away, a brown short gown, and brown serge petticoat, a blue short cloak unbound with a cap to it, and took off with her two striped callico long gowns, with some other cloathing. She has a mark on her breast, occasioned by being burnt. She speaks good English, and is rather more yellow than black, aged about 24 years old. Whoever takes up said Wench, and brings her to her master, living in Fair street, No. 3, shall receive the above reward. All persons are forbid harbouring the said Wench. John Carow.

N. B. The above Wench formerly belonged to Parson Burnet, on Long Island. [*Royal Gazette* (New York), February 13, 1782]

[359] Run away, the 23d of October last, from the subscriber, living in Hamilton township, Cumberland county, a servant Girl, born in Philadelphia, named Margaret Morris, about 15 years of age, of low stature, black hair, and squints with one eye; had on and took with her a white linen bonnet, an old striped linen short gown, one white linen ditto, an old striped lincey petticoat, a striped cotton ditto, and a pair of calfskin shoes. Whoever takes up said servant, and brings her home to her master, or secures her in any goal so that he may have her again, shall have Three Hard Dollars reward, and reasonable charges, paid by William Cowen. [*Pennsylvania Gazette*, March 6, 1782]

[360] Eight Dollars Reward. Run away from the subscriber, on Sunday evening last, a likely Negro Wench, nineteen years of age, named Charlottee, formerly the property of Captain Salter, she is somewhat pitted with the small pox, had on when she went away, a white gown and petticoat: Whoever takes up said Wench, and secures her so that her master can obtain her, shall receive the above reward, and all reasonable charges paid by me John Vanderhoven. [*Royal Gazette* (New York), March 6, 1782]

[361] Twenty Silver Dollars Reward. Ran away from the subscriber, living near Baltimore-Town, a negro girl, named Sarah, about 16 years of age; had on when she went away, a linsey short gown, an old blue quilted petticoat, an old castor hat, a tow linen apron, a blue and red handkerchief; she took with her an old riding skirt and lawn apron. Whoever takes up said Negro, or secures her, so that her master may have her again, shall have the above Reward if taken out of the state, or Eight Dollars if taken in this state, and all reasonable charges, paid by Benjamin Wells, jun. [*Maryland Journal*, April 23, 1782]

[362] Twenty Shillings Reward. Ran away from the subscriber, living at the three mile stone, on the Germantown road, an indented Servant Girl, named Elizabeth Jefry, eight years of age, black hair cut short before, black eyes, flat nose and round face: had on when she went away, a striped short gown, a brown linsey pettecoat and check apron pinned behind; she is concealed about the barracks with an intention to send her to her mother. Whoever apprehends said Runaway, and brings her to her master, shall have the above Reward and reasonable charges paid. Steward Catly. [*Pennsylvania Packet*, April 25, 1782]

[363] Run away on Friday the 10th instant, a middle sized Negro Wench named Phillis; had on when she went away, a brown strouding jacket, black shirt, cheque apron, blue stockings, and Men's shoes, simple in behavior. Whoever will bring her to the Owner at No. 32, John Street, shall receive Two Dollars reward. All persons are forbid harbouring or employing said Negro Wench, as she is a warranted property. [*Royal Gazette* (New York), May 15, 1782]

[364] Twenty Dollars Reward. Ran Away from the subscriber, living in the town of Richmond, a very likely Negro woman named Molly, lately the property of Mr. Edward Busbel, of Gloucester-town; she is much pitted with the small-pox, about twenty-two years old, and about five feet six inches high; had on when she went away, a Virginia cloth vest and petticoat, checked; she had with her a checked apron, a callico petticoat, and a pair of leather high-heeled country made shoes. I expect she will make towards

Williamsburg or Gloucester-town, as she came from those parts a few days ago. She had four horse-locks fastened on her legs when she went away. Whoever apprehends and delivers the said Negro to me, shall receive the above reward and reasonable charges, paid by Isaah Isaacs. [Hayes's *Virginia Gazette*, June 2, 1782]

[365] Run Away on Tuesday the 25th ultimo, a hearty young Negro Wench named Tenah, of the Hebo Country, about nineteen years of age, and yellow complexion; had on when she went away a white short gown and petticoat, a check apron and printed handkerchief. She was late the property of Mrs. Elizabeth Butler, and purchased at Public Sale the day before from John Davies, Esq, Sheriff. Any Person who will deliver her to the keeper of the Sugar House, or to the Subscriber, at No. 89, Broad-street, shall receive Twenty Dollars Reward from Gerald Fitzgibbon. [*Royal South Carolina Gazette*, July 9, 1782]

[366] Two Dollars Reward. Run away from the Subscriber, a young Negro Girl, about thirteen or fourteen years of age; had on when she went away, a white short gown, and black calimanco skirt, no cap, but a black bonnet; of a fair complexion, with three specks of the small pox on her nose, and has two of her upper teeth out, and a pair of gold bobs in her ears. I forwarn all masters of vessels or others from harbouring or concealing her at their peril. If any person will deliver her to her Mother, living at the White Hall, shall be paid the above reward, by me, Elizabeth Walker. [*Royal Gazette* (New York), August 3, 1782]

[367] Ran away from the subscriber, at Norwich Landing, a negro woman named Rose, slave for life, about 26 years old, lusty and fleshy, of a smiling countenance, shows her foreteeth when she laughs, wears a large roll on her hair combed back and a small woman's hat, had on or has with her a striped brocaded callico gown, with apron of the same new, two striped short linen loose ditto, one red callimanco skirt, one brown ditto, one pair of new sol'd cotton stockings, one pair of homemade ditto, leather shoes, some worn with white rands. Whoever will take up said slave, and return her to me the subscriber, shall have Ten Dollars reward, paid by me Abel Brewster. [*Connecticut Gazette*, August 22, 1782]

[368] Three Guineas Reward. Ran away, a negro wench named Peg, who formerly lived with Justice Campbell, at the Short Hills, in New Jersey, and lately with John D. Crimsheir, in Philadelphia. She is 29 years of age, low of stature, and strong made; she had on when she went away, a blue petticoat, striped short gown, a new black bonnet with red lining, and a pair of mens shoes. It is presumed that she is gone to Chatham in New Jersey, or else is concealed in this city, or some place near it, by some free Negroes or people's servants. All persons are therefore strictly forbid to harbour the said wench, or employ her, as they will not only be prosecuted for keeping her, but be sued for her work and labour. Whoever takes up the said wench, and secures her so that she may be had again, shall receive the above reward, and all expences, by applying to Eleazer Oswald, next door to the Coffee House in Market Street. [*New Jersey Journal*, September 11, 1782]

[369] Four Dollars Reward. Ran away from the subscriber, living in Front street, between Market and Arch streets, early last Saturday morning, an apprentice girl named Mary Oldham, between fourteen and fifteen years of age, of a small size, lisps very much, is apt to swear, her hair short before and generally stands up. She had on, when she went away, a short gown and petticoat of died linen, which had been washed, a tow shift, but neither shoes or bonnet. Whoever secures her, so that her master gets her again, shall have the above reward and reasonable charges. Justinian Fox. [*Pennsylvania Evening Post*, September 16, 1782]

[370] Four Dollars Reward. Ran away, on the morning of the 21st instant, from the subscriber, a servant girl, named Martha Thomson; has black hair, and is of a dark complexion. Had on when she went away, a brown, plain, linsey petticoat, a callico short-gown, with small white spots, a pair of men's shoes, a small black silk bonnet, and a black moreen petticoat. She snuffs, drinks and smokes. Whoever takes up said servant girl, and brings her to her master, on Levi Hollingsworth's wharf, at the sign of General Washington, shall have the above reward and all reasonable charges, paid by Matthew Hand. [*Independent Gazetteer* (Philadelphia), September 24, 1782]

[371] Ran away from the subscriber at Middlebush, in Somerset county, State of New Jersey, a mulatto wench, about fifteen years of age, five feet four or five inches high; had on when she went off a linen short gown and petticoat: Whoever takes up the said wench, and secures her, so that the owner may have her again, shall have Twenty Shillings reward, and all reasonable charges paid by Jeromus Rappelyea.

N. B. It is supposed she went off with the French troops. [*New Jersey Gazette*, November 20, 1782]

[372] Ran away from the Subscriber, in the Night of the Fifteenth Instant, a Wench, Half Indian and Half Negro, named Phoebe, Twenty Six Years of Age, large and strong, much pitted with the Small-Pox, has a remarkable piercing Eye, some Scars round her Neck and back, and is very talkative. Took with her one Calico Gown, one striped Linen Ditto, one Drugget Ditto, a black Cloak, &c. Whoever will bring said Wench to the Subscriber, shall have Two Guineas Reward; or whoever will give Information so that she may be had, shall be handsomely paid for their Trouble. James Dagget. [*Providence Gazette*, November 22, 1782]

[373] Ran away from the Subscriber, in the Evening of the 8th Instant, a Negro Wench named Lucy, about 21 Years of Age; took with her one Calico Gown one striped Linen Ditto, one green Calimanco Quilt, one blue Worsted Skirt, one dark Petticoat, one striped Kersey Ditto, one striped Linen Wrapper, one dark woollen Ditto, one red Broadcloth Cloak, one blue Silk Hat, one white Linen Apron, one checked Ditto, one blue woollen Ditto, &c. Whoever will bring said Wench to the Subscriber shall have Ten Dollars Reward, and all necessary Charges; or a reasonable Reward will be paid to any Person who will give Information where she is. John Rice. [*Providence Gazette*, December 12, 1782]

[374] Sixteen Dollars Reward. Ran away, about nine o'clock last evening, a yellow Negro Girl, named Jenny, about 20 years of age, 5 feet 4 inches high, smart and likely, country born; she took with her a bundle of cloaths, consisting of one light chintz gown, a small figure with red stripes, one dark ditto with a large flower and yellow stripes, seven yards of new stamped linen, a purple

Jenny, "a yellow Negro Girl," wears a chintz gown "with a large flower and yellow stripes," "a pink coloured moreen petticoat, a new black peelong bonnet," under "a chip hat trimmed with gauze and feathers," a white apron, and a "pair of blue worsted shoes with white heels;" she carries a piece of "new stamped linen, a purple flower and stripe." See advertisement 374 from the *New York Journal*, December 17, 1782. Illustration by Eric H. Schnitzer.

flower and stripe, a pink coloured moreen petticoat, a new black peelong bonnet, a chip hat trimmed with gauze and feathers, four good shifts, two not made up and two a little wore, four aprons, two white and two check, one pair of blue worsted shoes with white heels. She is very fond of dress, particularly of wearing queen's night-caps. She had in her shoes a large pair of silver buckles. It is probable that she has gone either to New York or Baltimore. Whoever secures the said Wench, so that her master may have her again, shall have the above Reward and all reasonable charges paid by David C. Claypoole, Printer in Market street, or the subscriber in the Northern Liberties. Levi Budd. [*Maryland Journal*, December 17, 1782]

1783

[375] Run away, on Thursday morning, the 13th instant, a stout Negro Wench, the property of Mrs. Mary Carey, named Nancy Blond: She had on a green baize wrapper, a light coloured petticoat, and a bundle of other clothes. Whoever will bring her to her Mistress at the Rose and Crown, in Queen street, shall receive Forty Shillings reward. It is ordered she shall be stopped at the Ferry, and all masters of vessels are warned not to take her on board. [*Royal Gazette* (New York), February 15, 1783]

[376] Ten Dollars Reward. Run away on the 14th instant, a Negro Woman named Lydia, aged about forty, Speaks Good English, is remarkably tall and stout made, has a large mark on her right cheek where she has been burnt; she had on her a blue negro cloth jacket and coat, a blue shalloon gown, a red and white cotton handkerchief round her head, a blue and white ditto about her neck, and a pair of men's shoes, and a ditto men's clowded stockings. She has belonged to Mrs. Derise, sen. and to Mr. Dalziel Hunter. The Reward will be paid on delivery of the said Wench, by Mr. McDowell, No 27 Broadstreet; and any person harbouring her after this notice will be prosecuted according to law. [*South-Carolina Weekly Advertiser*, February 19, 1783]

[377] Run Away, from the Subscriber on the 10th instant, a Mulatto, or Quadroon Girl, about 14 years of age, named Seth, but calls herself Sal, sometimes she says she is white and often paints

her face to cover that deception; she staid out of her master's house for two or three nights before she went off, and was seen dancing in a house, at or near the old barracks, where, it is probably, she is still lurking. She had on when she went off, a red baize jacket, petticoat, and high-heel'd shoes; she has black curled hair, and a large spot of the leprosy on her right side, she is well known in town, and particularly at the Fly-Market, for many wicked tricks. Two Dollars reward will be given to any person who will bring her home, or given information so that she may be found. All Masters of vessels, and others are forewarned not to harbour the said Mulatto Girl, as they shall answer at their peril. A. A. M'Kay, No. 27, Maiden Lane. [*Royal Gazette* (New York), March 15, 1783]

[378] Eight Dollars Reward. Run away from the subscriber, a Negroe Wench, called Jenny, about 25 years old, remarkably short and thick, and of a dark complexion: she has lost her under jaw foreteeth, is a little pitted with the small-pox, speaks tolerably well, and is commonly dressed in a brown woolen habit, or in woolen blue coat and jacket, and sometimes in a blue and white callicoe jacket. She went away last Wednesday. This is therefore to offer the above reward to any person who will apprehend the said wench and deliver to me, or to the Warden of the Workhouse: And a further reward of eight dollars will be paid to any person who will inform of her being harboured by a white person, and four dollars if harboured by a negroe, on conviction of the offender or offenders, forbidding all persons at their peril from carrying her off. Daniel Tanin. [*South Carolina Gazette*, March 22, 1783]

[379] Forty Shillings Reward. Run away from the subscriber, on the night of the 28th instant, a Servant Maid, named Elizabeth Gest, about 22 years of age, country born, of a pale complexion, middle sized, has lost her fore teeth, with short black hair, and fair skin; had on, when she went away, a striped linsey green and yellow petticoat, yellowish short gown, black silk bonnet, a cloth coloured cloak, without a cape, blue stockings, and low heeled leather shoes; she went off with an old soldier, lately come from camp, and calls himself John Pattenton, who has left a wife and child behind; he is a shabby looking fellow; had on, when he went

away, an old patched hat, old light coloured jacket and overalls, much patched, striped flannel shirt, and old shoes; he is about 5 feet 7 or 8 inches high, of a pale complexion, with lightish hair; says he is an Englishman born, and has been a soldier in the continental army. Whoever takes up and secures said servant in any goal, so that her master may have her again, shall have the above reward, paid by Benjamin Jones. [*Pennsylvania Gazette*, April 2, 1783]

[380] Ran away from the subscriber in January last, a Negro girl named Sarah, country born, about 17 years of age, about four feet four inches high, of a yellow complexion, full ey'd, her nose very large, and a ring in one of her ears, had on a blue wrapper, was lately taken up at the Salt ketchers with two other Negro girls, on her way to Georgia, and sent to Mrs. Main's Indian land, from whence she has made her elopement: Whoever will deliver her to me, or the wardens of the work-house in Charlestown, shall receive three Guineas reward with reasonable charges. Henry Leibert. [*South Carolina Gazette*, May 2, 1783]

[381] Eight Dollars Reward. Run away from the subscriber, living in West Nantmill township, Chester county, State of Pennsylvania, on the first instant, a Negroe Wench named Sall, about 30 years of age, tall and slender of stature, says she was born in Georgia; had on and took with her two linsey petticoats, striped blue and white, two linen shifts, one blue and white striped linsey bed gown, one copperas coloured ditto, one white ditto, both linen, one pair of new shoes made man's fashion, and without straps. It is supposed she has carried off some of her mistress's clothes, which are not here described. Whoever takes up said negroe, and secures her in any goal, so that her master may have her again, shall have the above reward, and reasonable charges, paid by John Graham. [*Pennsylvania Gazette*, May 7, 1783]

[382] Ran away from the subscriber, on Wednesday, the 7th instant, a servant girl, named Mary Brighten, 17 years of age; had on, and took with her, one striped short gown and petticoat, one pair white cotton stockings, two pair of high heeled shoes, and sundry other clothes taken out of the wash tub. Whoever secures

said servant, and delivers her to the common goal of Lancaster, shall have Six pence Reward. [*Pennsylvania Gazette*, May 21, 1783]

[383] Description of Charles Broescke, Quarter-Master to Colonel de Linsing's battalion of Hessian Grenadiers, who absconded since yesterday afternoon, and took with him the sum of Three hundred and forty pounds Sterling, Subsistence Money belonging to the above-mentioned regiment. He is about 40 years old, under the middle size, rather fat, a round full and pale face, short neck, his head bending forwards, not much hair, which is of a brown colour, and which he used to tie in a queue. Had on before he went away, a blue coat, with lappels, the buttons holes trimmed with a small silver lace, white under-cloaths, and boots. He had a connection with a young woman, named Sally Bunn, from Perth-Amboy, who may now perhaps be with him; she went to the Jersies on Saturday the 24th instant, is a good looking woman, of the middle size, about 22 years old, her face and features rather large, dark hair, had on a yellow silk, when she went away. All persons, civil and military, are desired to assist in apprehending the above deserter. [*Royal Gazette* (New York), May 31, 1783]

[384] Run away from the subscriber, on the 28th of March last, an apprentice girl, named Catherine Crout, of short stature, with long yellow hair, broad faced, and squints a little; had on, and took with her, an home made gown, white and yellow, one short ditto of the same, two lincey short gowns, two home spun shifts and two aprons, one black lincey petticoat, one red ditto, a red and white calicoe jacket and petticoat, a linen bonnet of a lye colour, with sundry other articles. Whoever takes up said girl, and secures her, so that her master may have her again, shall receive a reward of One Shilling, paid by Duncan Beard. [*Pennsylvania Gazette*, June 4, 1783]

[385] Eight Dollars Reward. Run Away from the subscriber, living in West Nantmill township, Chester county, on the 20th of May last, a likely, tall, strait and slender made Negroe Wench, named Sal, about 30 years of age, says that she was born in Augusta, in the State of Georgia, but lately from the State of New Jersey and Philadelphia; had on and took with her, a striped blue

and white linsey petticoat, one striped tow ditto, one striped linsey short gown, the sleeves pieced with a different kind of striped cloth, one linen striped copperas coloured ditto, one white ditto, one check apron, one tow ditto, a pair of old shoes made mens fashion, had neither hat nor bonnet when she went away, but a blue and white checked handkerchief which she wore about her head, will endeavour to pass for a free woman, pretty eloquent in speaking, very positive, and much addicted to lying. Whoever takes up and secures her, so as the owner may get her again, shall receive the above reward, and reasonable charges, paid by John Graham. [*Pennsylvania Gazette*, June 11, 1783]

[386] Run away from the Subscriber, living at No. 110, Water street, near the New Slip, a Negro Girl named Poll, about 13 years of age, very black, marked with Small Pox, and had on when she went away a red cloath petticoat, and a light blue short gown, home made. Whoever will take up and secure the said Girl, so that the owner may get her, shall be handsomely rewarded by Thomas Brinckley. [*Royal Gazette* (New York), June 14, 1783]

[387] Fifteen Dollars Reward. Run away on Friday the 13th instant, a negro wench named Luce, about 30 years of age, middling, or rather low in stature; her right cheek stained of a different colour from her natural black, carries her head remarkably high, and seems to have a difficulty to open her eyes, she is very noisy and quarrelsome in the streets; had on when she went away a green striped stuff gown that has been washed, a dark blue moreen petticoat, a gauze cap and pink ribbons, no hat, she had also with her a dark purple callicoe gown, she commonly goes by the name of Luce Price, from her having formerly lived with Edward Price, the pilot, on Cruger's wharf; she has been seen two or three times since she run away about the streets, the last time at the Fly Market, supposed to be going over the Ferry, where she sometimes used to run, as also to Harlaem and Shrewsbury: It is supposed she is lurking somewhere in this city, and is afraid to come home. Any person who will discover her to her master, at No. 49, the corner next to the Exchange, so that he may apprehend her shall receive the above reward; and if said wench will voluntar-

ily return home, her master will forgive her. All persons are cautioned not to conceal, harbour, or carry off said wench. [*New York Gazette*, June 29, 1783]

[388] Ran away from the subscriber, in Montgomery township, county of Philadelphia, and state of Pennsylvania, on the 20th of June last, a servant girl named Elisabeth Makever, about 17 years of age, tall and slender, of a swarthy complexion and squints. Had on when she went away, a gown and petticoat of striped blue linen and worsted, blue stockings and new shoes. Whoever takes her up, and brings her home again, shall receive half a dollar reward, from Samuel Hines. [*Freeman's Journal* (Philadelphia), August 6, 1783]

[389] Eight Dollars Reward. Run away on Sunday morning the 3d instant, a tall, stout negro wench and her child; the wench is named Lucy, the child Venus. The wench is very much pitted with the small pox, and her feet is so large that she is obliged to ware mens shoes. She took with her two short gowns, and two petticoats, one striped bottom short gown and a yellow ground callicoe one; one black petticoat and one other supposed green, either of which she wears. The child had on a tow cloth frock, has a scar on her shoulder, and is about 5 or 6 years old. Her mother is about 28 years. Whoever gives information to the printer so as the owner may have them again, shall receive the above reward. All persons are forewarned not to conceal, harbour or carry off the said wench and her child, as they will have to answer for it at their peril. [*New York Gazette*, August 18, 1783]

[390] A Negro Girl, about 12 years old, named Madlane, who arrived in this Town yesterday, strayed away, having on a striped Woollen Rapper, dark blue Petticoat, with white flowers, and was bare footed. Whoever will show her to No. 11, Little Queen Street, shall have Four Dollars for their trouble. [*Royal Gazette* (New York), October 3, 1783]

[391] Run away from the subscriber, on the 12th of September, 1783, a negro wench named Nancy; she is a tall, lusty, likely Wench, about 19 years of age, speaks slow, her feet are large and long, parrot toed, one of her lower front teeth is out; she was for-

merly the property of the Widow Nisbett, and Wadmelaw. Had on when she run away, an oznebrig short gown and petticoat, but perhaps she may change her apparel. All masters of vessels are forbid to harbour or carry her off. Whoever will deliver the said Negro Wench to the subscriber, or to the Warden of the Sugar-House, shall receive two Guineas reward, paid by the subscriber, at no. 186, King street. Thomas Eustace. [*South Carolina Gazette*, October 3, 1783]

[392] Five Pounds Reward. Run away, on Friday 19th September, a Negro Wench, named Kate, born in the family of Jacob Bennet, on Long Island, has lived with Mr. George Hunter and Ephraim Smith, of this City: She is very stout made, about 5 feet 9 or 10 inches high, of a light black, and likely face, without any particular marks, generally wears her hair very high and straight up, over a roll, with a great deal of pomatum, a great talker and shrill voice; took with her a variety of clothes, among which there was a Callico Short Gown, with the figure of horses, carriages, and soldiers, in blue and yellow colours, particularly a row of the latter round the bottom of it; and several caps, all with long ears. It is supposed to feign the name of Boyle, an Ensign in General De Lancey's corps. Whoever will apprehend and secure her, so that her master may get her, shall have the above reward, and all reasonable charges paid, by applying to the Printer, or No. 19, Crown street. [*Royal Gazette* (New York), October 22, 1783]

[393] Ran away from the Subscriber, last Night, a Negro Man, named Freeman, about 38 Years of Age, about 5 Feet 6 Inches high, stout and well made; had on a dark great Coat, with Horn Buttons, a grey Kersey Jacket, and took with him a Variety of other Cloathing. Also a Negro Wench, his Wife named Venus, about 32 Years of Age, tall and likely; took with her a red short Cloak, a black bonnet, a Cloth coloured Worsted Gown, and Plenty of other Cloathing. Whoever will take up and return said Negroes to their Master, shall have Ten Dollars Reward, and all reasonable Charges paid by Samuel Tomkins. [*Providence Gazette*, October 25, 1783]

[394] Run away from the subscriber, a Negro Wench called Hagar, and her daughter called Mary, Hagar is about 40 years of age, speaks very good English. Mary about 12 years of age, speaks good English, had on when she went away a green frize habit. Whoever apprehends and secures said negroes, so that the owner may get them, shall receive a Guinea reward for each. Any person or persons harbouring said negroes, many depend on being prosecuted according to law; a farther reward of Five Guineas will be given to any person who shall give information of either of the said negroes being harboured by any white persons, on conviction. Barnard Moses.

N. B. I was since informed the above negroes crossed Ashley River a few days ago, and suppose they are gone to Mr. William Stoutenburg's plantation, as her relations belong to him. All masters of vessels are forbid to harbour, or carry them off. [*South-Carolina Gazette*, November 4, 1783]

[395] Ran away, the 29th of July 1783, from the subscriber, living in Prince-George's county, near the Woodyard, a short thick mulatto wench named Phillis, thirty years of age, hath a large scar on one of her cheeks; had on, when she went away, an old shift, old white linsey petticoat, and short gown, with a black stripe round the back; I bought her of Mr. Robert Darnall, and she may pass for his property, may change her name and cloaths, and pass for a free woman. Two years ago she ran away and hired herself to Mr. John Wynn, of Prince George's county, as a free woman, by the name of Charity Maginnis, and likewise to Mr. Samuel Beary, of Charles county, by the name of Charity Swan. Whoever will deliver the said wench to me, shall receive four hard dollars if taken in this county; if in Charles or St. Mary's counties eight dollars; if a farther distance a reasonable satisfaction, paid by me Ignatius Hardy.

N. B. This same wench was sold for running away, and hath been very troublesome to me; she is a great liar and a rogue, and artful in passing with many idle tales in her own neighbourhood, pretending to be sent about my business, and at the same time is run away. She hath made away with several articles of my property for her own; they are too tedious to mention; therefore I desire all manner of persons to have no manner of dealings with her, nor to harbour her one hour except my note from this date hereafter, but take her and deliver her to me, and they shall receive the above reward.

N. B. I do hereby certify, that the said wench is a slave. Robert Darnall. [*Maryland Gazette*, November 13, 1783]

[396] Run away from the subscriber, a negro girl named Hannah, has a remarkable flat nose and thick lips; had on when she went away, a callico wrapper and a white flannel coat; she is very sly and artful, and will tell a plausible story. She is supposed to be harboured up the path. All masters of vessels and waggoners are forbid carrying her off, and they will be dealt with as the law directs; and whoever will deliver her to me, and No. 107, Meeting street, shall have a suitable reward. William Fair. [*South Carolina Weekly Gazette*, November 14, 1783]

[397] Ten Pounds Reward. Run away from the Subscriber, on Sunday night the 16th inst. a Negro Wench, named Isabel; had on when she run away, a short whitish Cloth Cloak, with a hood, about 5 feet 6 inches high, very black colour, speaks pretty thick. She was taken away by her Husband, a Negro Man, called Peter Longster, about 6 feet high, pretty stout, formerly lived with Col. Lutwyche, at Brooklyne Ferry, Long Island. Whoever will secure either of them, or give information to the Subscriber, or to William Bryan, at the Fly Market Stairs, so that he may get his property again, shall receive the above reward, and all reasonable charges paid. Edward Bardin, at Jamaica, Long Island. [*Royal Gazette* (New York), November 19, 1783]

[398] Five Pounds Reward. Run away from the subscriber at Delaware Mills, Bucks County, and State of Pennsylvania, two Negroes, the one named Jim, about five feet six or seven inches high, thirty years of age, well made, a smart active fellow, of a yellowish complexion, had on when he went away a light coloured coat with a red crape, brown jacket and overalls. The other a Wench, wife to Jim, about thirty years of age, small in stature, slow in motion and speech, some scars in her face, had on when she went away a striped linsey petticoat and short gown; they both have changes of cloaths. Whoever takes up and secures said

Negroes shall have the above reward and reasonable charges paid by Mark Bird. [*Political Intelligencer and New Jersey Advertiser*, November 25, 1783]

[399] Five Pounds Reward. Ran away last night, an Irish servant Girl, named Jenny Stevenson, about 21 years of age, has blue eyes and black hair, a tall, lusty, hearty, fresh looking wench, and came in the brig Recovery, Capt. Junkin, from Belfast, about nine weeks ago. Had on and took with her, a green skirt, dark calicoe short gown, white stockings, leather shoes with low heels, two striped lincey petticoats, a striped red calicoe short gown, and a black Barcelona handkerchief. Whoever takes up and delivers the said girl to the subscriber, shall have the above reward. John Dunlap. [*Pennsylvania Gazette*, December 17, 1783]

[400] Two Guineas Reward. Run away from the Subscriber, the 24th day of November last, a likely Negro Woman, named Sarah, brought up in the family of Mr. Deycay, deceased, where she went by the name of Clarender, about thirty years of age; she is pretty tall and slender made, her complexion being very black, has a remarkable wart on her right eye lash. Had on when she went away, a callicoe short gown, black skirt, and a black hat trimmed with edging, but as she has a great number of good cloaths, which she carried away with her, it is impossible to describe the dress she may now be in. It is supposed, that she is kept concealed some-where in this city, she having a great many relations and acquain-tances here. This is to forewarn all persons from harbouring her, as they will answer it at their peril. Any person who will apprehend the said Negro Woman, and secure her so that her mistress may have her again, shall receive the above reward, paid them by me, living at No. 385, Murray Street. Elizabeth Miller. [*New York Gazetteer*, December 17, 1783]

GLOSSARY

Note: During the time period covered by this book terminology was not standardized and printers used the terms given to them by the subscribers of advertisements. The definitions given here are intentionally short and general, and refer to the context of the advertisements. Many terms have other meanings, or meanings that are imprecise and debatable.

800: The number of threads per inch, usually used to describe fine linens for shifts and shirts.

BAIZE (BAYS): A coarse woolen cloth with a felt-like knap, often used for linings.

BANDANO: Bandana, a piece of cloth used as a handkerchief.

BARCELONA: A square made of twilled silk and used as a neck or pocket handkerchief.

BEARSKIN: A heavy woolen fabric with a shaggy nap.

BEAVER: Woolen felt used to make broad-brimmed hats, so called because it looked similar to beaver pelt.

BEDGOWN (see also GOWN, SHORT GOWN): A loosely-fitted gown extending to the mid-thigh or knee.

BIRD'S EYE: Fabric woven in such a way as to create diamond patterns with dots in the center, resembling birds' eyes. The pattern was caused by the weave, not by the color of the thread.

BLEACHER: A person or company that bleached natural linen to a white color.

BOMBAZEEN: A lightweight silken fabric sometimes used for mourning.

BRANCHES: A pattern resembling twigs or tree branches, woven into or printed onto the fabric.

BRISTOL STUFF: A woolen fabric made in Bristol, England.

BROADCLOTH: Fine, plain-weave woolen cloth with a felted finish, woven in wide widths.

BROWN LINEN: Natural, unbleached linen.

BUCKSKIN: The tanned hide of a deer or goat, used for clothing.

CALASH: A folding hood or bonnet.

CALICO: A plain-weave, lightweight, coarse cotton cloth either plain white or printed; originally from Calcutta.

CALIMANCO: A heavy worsted or woolen fabric with a plain weave and a glossy finish.

CAMBLET, CAMBLETEE: A fabric made to imitate an ancient fabric of camel's hair and silk; usually a wool and silk combination.

CAMBRICK: A fine plain-weave linen.

CAPUCHIN: A cloak with a hood.

CARDINAL: A short cloak, often hooded.

CARVED: Having designs cut or engraved.

CASTOR: Felt made from beaver fur.

CAUL: The back part of a cap or bonnet, that encloses the hair.

CHAIN: Alternative name for the warp threads.

CHARLOTTE: Based on the context, probably a specific printed or woven pattern of fabric for a gown.

CHECK: Plain weave fabric of linen, cotton, flannel or a mix thereof, with a pattern of squares formed by using different colors in the weave.

CHINTZ (CHINTS): A fabric printed with flowers or other designs and often wax glazed, usually cotton but sometimes linen.

CHIP: Long, thin wood shavings that could be woven, used to make hats similar to straw hats.

CLOCKS: Designs knitted into or embroidered on the ankle area of stockings.

CLOTH: General term usually referring to a heavy woolen fabric.

CLOUDED: Amorphous pattern created by knitting with two colors, usually in stockings.

COAT: Often used as a short-form of "petticoat."

COATING: Fabric used to make coats, usually a long-knapped wool.

COOLER: A loose sleeved garment with a drawstring neckline, usually for children.

COPPERAS: A pigment used for coloring textiles that yielded shades of bluish-green.

COUNTRY CLOTH: Either homespun fabric, or fabric made in the colonies, of linen, cotton, wool or a blend thereof.

CROSS-BARRED: Patterned with widely-spaced intersecting stripes of different colors.

DAMASK (DAMASCUS): An elaborately-patterned printed silk fabric.

DIAPER: Fabric of linen, cotton or a blend, with various patterns woven into it.

DICED: Having a pattern of squares woven into it.

DIMITY: Lightweight linen or cotton fabric with stripes or patterns woven into it.

DO.: Abbreviation for "ditto", that is, the same as the one before.

DOWLAS: Coarse, plain-weave linen fabric.

DRUGGET: A woolen which might also contain some silk or linen, used primarily in work clothes.

DUFFIL: An inexpensive heavy woolen fabric with a shaggy finish.

DURANT: A stout, durable, ribbed woolen fabric.

ERMINE: A white-pelted animal similar to a weasel; the pelt was valued as a trimming material.

EVERLASTING: Heavy, tightly twill-woven woolen cloth, sometimes two-tone with geometric designs woven in.

FEARNAUGHT: A heavy woolen fabric with a long pile, often used for bad-weather garments.

FERRET: Ribbon or tape used for binding.

FIGURED: Fabric having a pattern of shapes or figures printed on it or woven into it.

FILLING: Alternative name for the weft threads.

FLAG: Fabric printed with a design reminiscent of a flag.

FLANNEL: A medium weight woolen or worsted fabric with a smooth nap, twill or plain-weave.

FLAX: Plant with stalks bearing fiber used to make thread, or the thread made from the flax plant.

FLOUNCES: A part of a garment shaped so as to swell and shake.

FRIZE: A heavy coarse woolen fabric with a nap on one side.

FUSTIAN: A coarse, sturdy twilled fabric made from cotton and flax.

GAMBADOES: Leggings worn on the lower leg above the shoes, creating an effect similar to boots.

GAOL: Jail. Also spelled goal.

GAUGER: An official who verified weights and measures of goods.

GAUSE: A light, transparent fabric of silk or linen.

GIMP: An open trim material made from twists of silk, worsted or linen with a wire stiffener, worked to form a pattern.

GOAL: Jail. Also spelled gaol.

GROUND: The background color of a printed or patterned fabric.

GOWN (see also SHORT GOWN, BED GOWN): Garment made with a fitted upper body, sleeves, and a long skirt.

HALF-THICKS: A coarse weave woolen fabric.

HANDKERCHIEF: A square or triangular piece of lightweight fabric used by women to cover the neck, shoulders and bosom.

HEMP: Plant bearing coarse fibers used to make linen fabric and rope, or the fabric made from the hemp plant.

HOMESPUN: Fabric woven from yarn that was not commercially spun or processed.

HOLLAND: A glazed linen fabric, originally manufactured in Holland.

HUMHUM: A thick, strong cotton fabric.

INDIA: Fabric imported from India, or made in imitation thereof.

INST.: Instant, in the current month.

JACKET (JACKCOAT): A fitted upper-body garment with sleeves, and skirts varying in length from waist to mid-thigh.

JEAN: A twill-weave fabric made from a mix of linen, cotton or a blend thereof.

KENTING (KENTON): A fine linen named because it was widely manufactured in Kent, England.

KERSEY: A coarse, twilled woolen fabric, often ribbed, with a short nap.

LAWN: A delicate, light-weight linen fabric.

LEGHORN: Fine wheat-straw plaiting used for making hats.

LINEN: Fabric made of the fibers of flax or hemp. The thread count is sometimes specified, for example, "900 linen."

LINEN SHEER: A large scissor used for cutting linen fabric.

LINSEY, LINCEY: A coarse, loosely woven fabric of wool and linen, also called linsey-woolsey.

LINSEY WOOLSEY: A coarse, loosely woven fabric of wool and linen, also called linsey.

LIST: Fabric colored in streaks.

LUTESTRING: Also lustring, a glossy silk fabric.

MANTUA: A type of loose-fitting gown open in the lower front to show the petticoats.

MAP: Fabric printed with a design reminiscent of a map.

MECKLENBURG: A fancy glazed linen fabric.

MIXT (MIXED): Yarn made by twisting different colored fibers together.

MODE: A plain-weave light silk fabric.

MOREEN: A plain-weave linen fabric with a stamped or waved finish.

MUSLIN: A lightweight cotton fabric.

NANKEEN: A plain-weave cotton material, yellowish in color, originally made in Nanking, China, and later imitated in England.

NAP: A shaggy surface finish of a fabric, usually wool.

NEAT'S LEATHER: Leather from the hide of a cow, as opposed to that from a goat, deer or other animal.

NEGRO CLOTH: A coarse homespun fabric of wool, linen or cotton.

OZNABRIG (OZENBRIGS, OSNABRUG): A coarse fabric made of woven flax or hemp, often unbleached.

PADUASOY: A rich, heavy silk fabric with a pattern woven into it.

PASTEBOARD: Stiff material formed by pressing layers of paper and adhesive together and molding it into shapes.

PATCH: Based on the context, possibly a chintz fabric.

PEELONG (PEELING): A silken fabric imported from China.

PERSIAN: A thin, plain silk fabric.

PETTICOAT (COAT): A loose garment tied around the waist and hanging to the calves or lower, worn as an outer or under garment; also, that part of a gown which hangs below the waist.

PINCHBECK: An imitation gold made from zinc and copper, named for the British jeweler who developed it.

PINCKED: Worked with small holes or eyelets.

PLAID (PLAD): A coarse woolen fabric, sometimes with a pattern of intersecting stripes.

PLAINS: Plainly woven cloth usually of wool.

PLUSH: A cloth composed of woolen threads woven with cotton, silk, wool or mohair, with a nap longer and softer than velvet.

POCKET: A cloth bag tied around the waist and worn on the side, for carrying personal items.

POMPADOUR: A rich purple color, or a broadcloth of this color.

POPLIN: A fabric made with a silk warp and a worsted weft.

PUMPS: Thin-soled, light shoes

QUILT: A garment made in a quilted fashion, having an inner layer stitched between outer layers of fabric.

RAPPING: As used in advertisement 140, the meaning is not known.

ROCCOLO: Roquelaure, a close-fitting knee-length cloak.

ROLLER: Cylinder used for shaping hair.

ROLLS: A coarse unbleached fabric made of flax or hemp.

ROMALL: A silk or cotton handkerchief imported from India.

RUG: A coarse woolen fabric with a shaggy finish.

RUSSIA: Any hemp linen (as opposed to flax linen) product, regardless of where it was produced, so-called because it was widely produced in Russia.

SACK: A type of fitted gown with a long skirt.

SARSNET: A thin, soft silk fabric.

SATIN: A silk fabric with a smooth, shiny finish.

SERGE: A twill-weave wool made with worsted thread, sometimes with silk or woolen warp.

SHAG: A heavy woolen fabric with a long nap.

SHALLOON: A thin, cheap twill-woven wool fabric.

SHEEP'S BLACK: Yarn made from natural colored wool of black sheep, often dark brown rather than black.

SHEETING: A plain-weave fabric of linen, hemp or cotton.

SHIFT: A woman's undergarment similar to a shirt.

SHORT GOWN (see also GOWN, BED GOWN): A fitted gown with skirts extending only to mid-thigh or knee length.

SKIRT: The portion of a gown, jacket or coat that extends below the waist; also, a petticoat.

SPRIGS, SPRIGGED (SPRINGS): Patterns resembling leaves or twigs, woven into or printed onto the fabric.

STAMPED: Having a design that was printed or stamped onto the fabric.

STAYS: An upper-body undergarment, fitted and stiffened.

STOMACHER: An ornamental piece of fabric worn on the front of the body.

STROUDING: A woolen fabric named for the river Stroud in England.

STUFF (STUFT): A general term for worsted wool fabrics.

SURTOUT: A large coat worn over all other clothing.

SWANSKIN: A fine woolen cloth of plain weave; the name was sometimes applied to fleecy cotton.

TAFFETY: A stiff, plain-weave silk fabric with a shiny finish.

TAMMY: A strong, lightweight fabric woven with a cotton warp and a worsted weft.

THREAD: Linen fibers spun into lengths for sewing or knitting, as opposed to yarn made from wool; the term is sometimes used to describe linen fabric.

TICKEN: A strong twill-weave linen fabric, often with stripes.

TIPPET: A scarf-like garment worn around the neck.

TOW (TOWCLOTH): A cheap, coarse, usually unbleached fabric made from short flax or hemp fibers.

TRAIN: Part of a gown that trails behind along the ground.

TWILL: A weaving technique that produced strong cloth with the appearance of a diagonal pattern in the weave.

ULT.: Ultimate, in the previous month.

VIRGINIA CLOTH: American-made fabric of cotton, linen, wool or a blend thereof.

WAISTCOAT: A jacket without sleeves, worn by women under a gown.

WALLET: A long bag with the opening in the middle, so that it could be slung over the shoulder with goods hanging in each end.

WARP (WARPING): The threads running lengthwise on a loom, and along the length of the woven fabric.

WEFT: Also woof, the threads running across the warp of woven fabric.

WHALEBONE: Stiffener made from the baleen of whales.

WOOLEN: Fabric or yarn made from short wool fibers carded and spun.

WORSTED: A type of yarn made by combing wool to remove short fibers and align the long ones, so named because it was widely produced in Worstead, England.

WRAPPER: A loose-fitting one-piece garment with sleeves and a long petticoat.

This glossary is compiled from the following sources:

Blacks Who Stole Themselves: Advertisements for Runaways in the Pennsylvania Gazette, 1728-1790. Billy G. Smith and Richard Wojtoowicz. Philadelphia: University of Pennsylvania Press, 1989.

Clothing and Textiles in New Jersey, 1776-1782: A study based on the New Jersey Archives, Newspaper Extracts, Second Series, Volumes 1-5. Michael Cleary. Plainfield, NJ: privately printed by the author, 1976.

A Dictionary of the English Language. Samuel Johnson. London, 1755.

Had on and Took with Him: Runaway Indentured Servant Clothing in Virginia, 1774-1778. Bryan P. Howard. Doctoral Dissertation, Texas A&M University, 1996.

Textiles in America, 1650-1870. Florence M. Montgomery. New York: W. W. Norton & Company, 1984.